T4-ATW-195

CROSSCURRENTS *Modern Critiques*

CROSSCURRENTS *Modern Critiques*

Harry T. Moore, *General Editor*

Herbert Lindenberger

Georg Büchner

WITH A PREFACE BY

Harry T. Moore

Carbondale

SOUTHERN ILLINOIS UNIVERSITY PRESS

To My Mother

Library of Congress Catalog Card Number 64–16355
Printed in the United States of America
Designed by Andor Braun

PREFACE

WHY A VOLUME on George Büchner (1813–37) in a series which calls itself Crosscurrents/Modern Critiques? Well, who can say where the modern begins? We were happy a few years ago to publish a good book on Mikhail Lermontov (1814–41), whose novel A Hero of Our Times (1840) is so much a part of our own time; to such modernistic writers as James Joyce and Boris Pasternak, Lermontov was a living figure, and they acknowledged their indebtedness to him. In the same way, Büchner is really "a new man," belatedly discovered. So, in our series he goes in among Joyce, Dreiser, Beckett, cummings, Durrell, O'Neill, and others who are modern by date as well as by temper.

Herbert J. Muller in The Spirit of Tragedy (Knopf, 1956) sees Büchner as one of the fathers of "modern realistic tragedy" in Woyzeck and Danton's Death. "It is manifestly unrealistic to believe that in modern nations any hero can restore social order or redeem his fellows by a sacrificial death, any more than America was restored or redeemed by the assassination of Abraham Lincoln. The most obvious tragedy of our times is that millions of people have been helpless victims of still more terrible historic fatalities, in economic depressions and world wars. Büchner accordingly forces the basic issue of modern realistic tragedy: whether on such terms man can retain the essential of tragic faith," as the protagonist does in Danton's Death. And George Steiner, in The Death of Tragedy (Knopf, 1961), finds Woyzeck "the first real tragedy of low life," and Büchner's work of the same "order of enrichment" as Van Gogh (who "has taught the eye to see the flame within the tree") and Schönberg (who "has brought to the ear new areas of possible delight"). Büchner "revolutionized the language of the theater and challenged definitions of tragedy which had been in force since Æschylus. By one of those fortunate hazards which sometimes occur in the history of art, Büchner came at the right moment. There was crucial need of a new conception of tragic form, as neither the antique nor the Shakespearean seemed to accord with the great changes in modern outlook and social circumstances. Woyzeck filled that need. But it surpassed the historical occasion, and much of what it revealed is as yet unexplored."

Herbert Lindenberger makes some of those explorations in the present book, the first full-length study of Büchner in English. In setting the scene for Mr. Lindenberger, I have felt justified, in quoting Messrs. Muller and Steiner, to whom he does not refer. He himself says so much about Büchner—his life and work and meaning—that it is difficult for the writer of a preface to add anything. Mr. Lindenberger takes you at once into the subject and keeps you there for about two hundred pages of what I find to be unalloyed critical delight.

I can then devote the rest of this preface to saying one or two things about Mr. Lindenberger. I first had the pleasure of meeting him through the medium of the (London) Times Literary Supplement. That was in London in the summer of 1958. The TLS kindly printed a letter of mine saying that I was editing a Lawrence critical anthology, A D. H. Lawrence Miscellany, and would be glad to consider any contributions sent to my London address at that time. Just as an unenclosed parenthesis—to give you some idea of the perils to which editors and even preface writers run into—I may mention that, two years later in England, I met one of those provincial schoolteachers who, though latecomers into the Lawrence vineyard, think Lawrence is their special property; he asked me rather huffily why there were so many American critics in the book, whose American edition had been published by Southern Illinois University Press in 1959. I pointed out that there were a number of English writers; I mentioned that I had asked A. Alvarez for permission to reprint an essay of his, had requested Christopher Hassall to write one, and so on; above all, I pointed out that I had invited contributions via England's most famous literary publication, the TLS. What more could one do? Yet that same provincial schoolteacher wangled a review of the English edition of the Miscellany (Heinemann, 1961), and groused because not enough British critics were represented! Perhaps the next time such a book is contemplated, its editors should wander through Soho, Bloomsbury, and Chelsea, to say nothing of the principal streets of redbrick-university towns, carrying large placards.

Anyhow, Herbert Lindenberger was one of those who read the letter in the TLS. He was then in London and wrote to me, and we met and discussed his essay on Lawrence and Wordsworth which later appeared in the Miscellany (and was one of the pieces highly spoken of in a TLS review of the book). Herbert Lindenberger in those days—and he may still wear it—had a jutting red beard, a Lawrencean touch. He had been a Fulbright Fellow in Austria a few years before, and he certainly knew a great deal about romanticism, English and European, as the present book demonstrates. I can remember discussing these matters with him on a Sunday-afternoon walk across the middle of London, from Marylebone through Hyde Park and into Chelsea.

A few weeks later, in Vence, Alpes-Maritimes, I had the great pleasure of meeting Gordon Craig, almost a lifelong hero of mine, and a man with whom I had some delightful chats that summer and again in 1960. He was a spectacular figure in his late eighties, wearing a white gown and looking about with the glare of an eagle coming from behind his great beak of a nose. He was passionately interested in obtaining Dutch cigars, which were hard to get in France, and he asked that if I had any friends coming to Vence, would I request them to bring him some Dutch cigars? One friend who went to see Craig, once, brought a scarf, which was quite a success. Then Herbert Lindenberger, who was going to the Riviera, went to elaborate trouble to obtain several packages of Dutch cigars. But when he arrived at Vence he learned from Gordon Craig's daughter that her father was in a hospital at Nice. Herbert went down there, and upon reaching the hospital was told that Craig was sleeping. But the sister told him to go on into the room and wait until the patient woke up. Herbert did so, and after a while when Craig opened his eyes and saw the red-bearded figure sitting nearby, he sat up in bed and roared, "What are you doing here?" He kept on roaring; there were alarums and excursions; but Craig was finally pacified when the visitor's mission was explained. The man supposedly ill at last accepted the cigars, in a happy mood, and immediately lighted and began smoking one of them.

"But for a few moments," Herbert Lindenberger wrote to me, "the old boy was playing Lear as it is all too seldom played and as it always should be played." That's pretty good; that's the way people should write letters. Similarly, I think that Herbert Lindenberger knows how to write books as they should be written. The pages that follow will bear me out.

HARRY T. MOORE

Southern Illinois University
July 4, 1964

CONTENTS

INTRODUCTION

THOUGH HIS plays have been available in various translations since 1927, in English-speaking countries Georg Büchner is still known chiefly for the fact that one of his works inspired Alban Berg's celebrated opera *Wozzeck.* The present book, the first full-length critical study of Büchner's works directed primarily to the English-speaking reader, attempts to introduce him through a detailed discussion of his four extant works and an analysis of their relation to earlier and later literary traditions. There have been some fine introductory essays in English on Büchner's career, most notably that of Michael Hamburger in his book *Reason and Energy* (London, 1957). A. H. J. Knight's book, *Georg Büchner* (Oxford, 1951), through its extended quotations in German and its attempt to survey all facets of Büchner's life with equal intensity, is essentially a background guide for the professional student of German literature.

The assumption which underlies this book is that the most effective way to introduce Büchner is through a critical examination of the works themselves. Since German is no longer, as it was a century ago, the second language of serious readers in English-speaking countries, I have quoted from Büchner in English translation. At times the reader will have to take my comments on a passage on faith, for Büchner, if nothing else, was a great master of language, and some of his most powerful moments elude even the most sensitive translator.

The translations quoted are as follows: John Holmstrom's of *Danton's Death*, in *The Modern Theatre*, ed. Eric Bentley, vol. V (New York: Doubleday, 1957); Eric Bentley's of *Leonce and Lena*, in *From the Modern Repertoire*, ed. Bentley, Series III (Bloomington, Ind.: Indiana U. Press, 1956); Michael Hamburger's, of *Lenz*, in *Partisan Review*, XXII (1955), 31–46, 133–42; and Theodore Hoffman's, of *Woyzeck*, in *The Modern Theatre*, vol. I (1955). On occasion I have altered a word or two in a quotation for the sake of a more literal rendering; my changes are all indicated by square brackets.

I am grateful to my colleagues Donald G. Daviau, Thomas R. Edwards, Frederick J. Hoffman, Douglass S. Parker, and Ada H. Schmidt, all of the University of California, Riverside, and to Michael Hamburger, of the University of Reading, England, and Egon Schwarz, of Washington University, for helpful suggestions on revising the manuscript. I should also like to extend my thanks to each of the following: to the administration of the University of California, Riverside, for granting me a sabbatical leave in the fall semester of 1962, and a leave of absence in the spring semester of 1963, to complete the writing of this book; to the Committee on Research of this university for funds for clerical assistance; to Mrs. Myra Boitin for typing the manuscript; and to my wife, Claire F. Lindenberger, for her advice throughout my work on this project.

HERBERT LINDENBERGER

Rome
June 14, 1963

Georg Büchner

1 THE BIOGRAPHICAL BACKGROUND

GEORG BÜCHNER, who died in 1837 at the age of twenty-three, is perhaps the only German writer before our own century who speaks directly to our time without the need of mediation. Germany has produced greater, more comprehensive writers, Goethe and Hölderlin, for instance, but these can reveal themselves to us only when we are prepared to recognize the historical circumstances which separate their world from ours. It seems no accident that Büchner's work was scarcely known at all until the end of his own century; indeed, his closeness to us is largely due to the fact that his themes and techniques anticipated much that is peculiar to the literature of our time.

Within the two years that encompass his career as a writer, Büchner wrote five works: two tragic dramas, *Danton's Death* and *Woyzeck*, each strikingly different from the other in subject and dramatic method, the second, in fact, a radical development from the already revolutionary method of the earlier play; a romantic comedy, *Leonce and Lena*, whose essentially despairing theme confounds the traditional comic conventions which it appears rigorously to pursue; and a story, *Lenz*, one of the first examples of European narrative fiction to demonstrate a method for the portrayal of introspective experience. The fifth work, a play based on the life of the Venetian wit Pietro Aretino, was never recovered from Büchner's literary remains.

Büchner's literary projects represent only one of several pursuits to which he dedicated himself during his brief life.

In the year that preceded the writing of his first play, while he was a student at the University of Giessen, in Hesse, he organized a revolutionary conspiracy against the oppressive Hessian government. Attempting to incite the Hessian peasantry to revolt, he composed a pamphlet, *The Hessian Messenger*, which, though it exercised no discernible effect on the *status quo*, retains an honorable place in the history of German political literature. *Danton's Death* was written while he lived in hiding from the Hessian police after the conspiracy had been broken up. His remaining works, all written after he had fled Germany, were composed in his spare time while he was working on his doctoral dissertation in Strasbourg and starting a career as lecturer at the University of Zurich. His literary works were forced to share in the creative energies he expended on his thesis, written in French, on the nervous system of the barbel fish, and his formal trial lecture at Zurich, on the cranial nerves. His death, of typhus, cut short what his university colleagues judged an auspicious beginning of a scientific career and what a small group of friends recognized as an equally auspicious beginning of a literary career.

ii

The Germany in which Büchner grew up was reactionary in its politics, idealistic in its philosophy, Romantic in its literary credo. He felt himself at odds with all these tendencies, and his antipathies are strongly reflected in his work. German philosophy, for instance, in the first part of the nineteenth century was dominated by a series of ornate idealistic systems, beginning with those of Kant and Fichte and culminating in Hegel's grand-style dialectic. Büchner had no patience with ideas that seemed to him to lack connection with the real world; he symbolized his attitude in *Leonce and Lena* in the figure of King Peter, who runs almost naked about his room ridiculously mouthing phrases about things-in-themselves, attributes, and categories, while looking for his clothes.

Büchner maintained a similarly skeptical attitude toward most of the literature of the period. By the time he had finished school the major writers of the Romantic school were either dead or, with the exception of Eichendorff, had long since completed their significant work. The basic values of later German Romanticism—Catholicism, nationalism, medievalism, transcendence of the everyday world—could only have gone against Büchner's grain; its styles and attitudes had, moreover, grown stale by his time. The writings of Hölderlin and Kleist, which stand outside the Romantic framework and were little appreciated in his day, were not commented upon by him. One of his few recorded remarks on contemporary literature attacks two derivative poets, Ludwig Uhland and Gustav Schwab, for "reaching back into the Middle Ages" instead of concerning themselves with present-day reality.[1] He felt almost as uncomfortable with the only organized opposition to Romanticism, the so-called Young Germany group of the 1830's, whom he condemned for the primarily theoretical nature of their liberalism. The only era of German literature with which Büchner felt any real affinities was the Storm-and-Stress period of the 1770's, characterized as it was by social realism, rebelliousness against stale literary forms, and a general explosive exuberance. Among his few literary forebears for whom he expresses admiration are such writers of the '70's as the young Goethe, the poet and dramatist Johann Michael Reinhold Lenz (an incident from whose life became the subject of Büchner's one piece of narrative prose), and, above all, Shakespeare, who, for the Storm-and-Stress writers and for Büchner was the arch-poet of real life in its fullness and variety.

The repressive political atmosphere of Büchner's native Hesse was more or less typical of the atmosphere of the various German states. After Napoleon's downfall the Grand Duke of Hesse, like the other petty monarchs of central Europe, attempted to re-establish the autocratic regime of an eighteenth-century ruler. Although he granted his people a constitution in 1820, it was of so conservative a nature that his traditional rights were scarcely impinged upon. In parts of Hesse the local nobility were still able to exact feudal duties from a peasantry which had scarcely risen above the condition of serfs. Oppressive taxes, together with a series of bad harvests during the post-Napoleonic period, reduced the peasants throughout Hesse to an increasingly intolerable state of poverty. The world which Büchner saw around him as he grew up was one of seemingly hopeless political and economic stagnation—a backward world, moreover, which would either beat a young man into submissive conformity or, as happened with Büchner, incite him to rebellion.

Büchner was born October 17, 1813, the same year as Napoleon's defeat at Leipzig. His father, Ernst Büchner, had been a military doctor with Napoleon's armies and throughout his life, though his sympathies could better be described as liberal than revolutionary, he remained essentially free-thinking and Francophile, with nostalgia for the expansive world he remembered before the Restoration. When Georg was born the father was practicing as a physician in the small town of Goddelau, near Darmstadt, the Hessian capital, to which the family moved three years later. Georg was the oldest of six children, all of whom but one—a sister who devoted herself to household duties—were to become prominent in German professional and intellectual life. Indeed, the three chief preoccupations of Georg's later life—his political, literary, and scientific interests—were all nurtured in one way or another in the family household. As a result of the father's political sentiments Georg early learned to think of the French Revolution as the most significant event of modern times. Georg's paternal ancestors had by family tradition entered the medical profession, and it was only natural that Georg, as firstborn, should follow suit; moreover, the anatomical display and laboratory which the elder Büchner kept in his home may well have awakened Georg's scientific curiosity at an early age. The mother, Caroline Reuss Büchner, was deeply religious and interested in poetry and folk songs; since she supervised Georg's early education, his literary sensibilities were doubtless developed by her in the same way that his scientific orientation was developed by his father. Despite the parents' differences in interests and temperament the family atmosphere remained relatively happy and secure; indeed, one can discern nothing in Büchner's family background to account for the development of one of the most despairing writers of world literature.

In 1822 Georg was sent to a private institute in Darmstadt and three years later entered the local *Gymnasium*, where he received the standard classical education of the time. He was an alert, conscientious student; the report written by the *Gymnasium* at the time of Georg's graduation records his success in all subjects except mathematics and makes a point of his independence of thought in his classes in religion. According to the testimony of two school-friends, Büchner's early literary interests extended widely through various literatures, but his major enthusiasm as an adolescent was directed to folk poetry, Shakespeare, and Goethe's *Faust* (of which little more than Part I had been published at the time); his antipathy to Schiller, whom he found too "rhetorical," was established equally early. Büchner's extant school essays reveal an articulate mastery of school rhetoric; one essay in particular, a passionately argued defense of suicide, is notable for its thesis that those who "commit suicide as a result of physical or psychological sufferings do not actually kill themselves, but can be said to die essentially of an illness." [2]

In 1831, the year he completed his secondary training, Büchner entered the University of Strasbourg, which his father had chosen for him for several reasons—the high quality of its medical school, in which Büchner matriculated; the presence in Strasbourg of his mother's cousin, the theologian Eduard Reuss; and, perhaps most important, the atmosphere of French culture to which he would be exposed. The two years which Büchner spent in Strasbourg during this, his first stay there, were probably the happiest of his life. He quickly made contacts around the university and joined a student club, the "Eugenia." Among his friends in the club were two brothers, August and Adolph Stöber, theology students and folklore enthusiasts; Büchner later drew liberally from their collection of Alsatian folksongs for his dramatic works, and he is also indebted to the Stöbers for the source material for *Lenz*.

In Strasbourg he lodged in the home of a pastor, Johann Jakob Jaeglé, to whose daughter, Minna, he became secretly engaged. Although Minna is not likely to have shared his free-thinking views, his few extant letters to her reveal a warm respect, and they also suggest that Minna, who was three years his senior, helped fulfill a strongly expressed need for affection and security. They waited until 1834 to announce their engagement and maintained their attachment until Büchner's death, which occurred before he was sufficiently independent—at least by nineteenth-century definition—to assume the responsibilities of marriage.

Büchner's Strasbourg years played a crucial role in his political development. For one thing, though Büchner had little enough respect for the government of Louis Philippe, he could observe in France a degree of freedom and prosperity that contrasted markedly with the conditions he had known in Hesse. Strasbourg, moreover, with its predominantly German-speaking population, was full of refugees who had fled the various German states during one uprising or another. More important still, Büchner in all likelihood participated in the activities of a French secret political group, the "Society for the Rights of Man," whose Strasbourg branch was notorious not only for its republican ideas but for its egalitarian economic sentiments. Unlike German political groups, which were made up largely of university students and were rarely so radical, the Society sought support and participation from workingmen. Whereas German conspiracies were usually *ad hoc* groups which broke up soon after they had staged an uprising, the Society, which was formed soon after the Revolution of 1830, was a closely knit network which maintained headquarters in Paris and nurtured long-range plans for another, more thorough-going revolution. If Büchner's observations in Strasbourg helped shape his later political career, his letters of the period also reveal the essential skepticism with which he was to treat political themes in his literary works. Thus, he uses the term "theater piece" (*Komödie*) to describe an enthusiastic demonstration in which he had participated to honor a leader of the unsuccessful Polish uprising of 1830. Another letter satirizes a young follower of St. Simon for his unrealistic utopianism. "If anything can help in our time, it is violence," he writes his parents.[3] Yet he was never to tell them of his own revolutionary activities and, in fact, even promised them to keep out of politics.

In 1833 Büchner reluctantly transferred to the University of Giessen in acquiescence with a Hessian law that required citizens of the grand duchy to acquire at least two years of their advanced training in the local university. The world he entered in Giessen was in every way a contrast to the Strasbourg world he had left behind. The town was small and provincial, and even the surrounding landscape, as Büchner described it in a letter to Minna, was "mediocre." [4] Instruction in the biological sciences was inferior to that in Strasbourg; indeed, Büchner was later to paint a mercilessly satirical portrait of one of his professors in *Woyzeck*. Student life, moreover, lacked the liveliness he remembered among his friends in the Eugenia group. One of his fellow students at Giessen, in turn, later described him as arrogant and aloof, a perpetual observer, though the few friends he chose to make described him in far warmer terms. Soon after he entered the University he came down with an attack of meningitis and spent some weeks in his parents' home to convalesce; in two letters to his fiancée probably written shortly after his illness he expresses sentiments which, in language and tone, resemble some of the most despairing feelings voiced by characters in his literary works.[5]

Büchner's disillusionment was nurtured still further by the fact that political conditions in Hesse had worsened considerably in recent years. A new grand duke who assumed the throne in 1830 attempted to pay off the royal family's sizable private debts by new taxes from the already overburdened peasantry. After the Parisian Revolution of

1830 the Hessian parliament began to show signs of opposition to the regime, but the grand duke quickly disbanded it and arranged for elections which could assure him of a loyal parliamentary following. The chief power in the land came to rest in the duke's trusted minister, Du Thil, who tightened his rule into that of a virtual police state.

"Political conditions here could drive me insane," Büchner wrote to one of his Strasbourg friends in December, 1833; [6] within a month or two he had begun actively to do something about them. Sometime in early 1834, soon after his recovery from meningitis, he organized a Society for the Rights of Man, named and modelled after the French organization. The group was based in Giessen, but Büchner also established a Darmstadt branch some months after. The members of the group included several of Büchner's fellow students, but, like its French counterpart, the society also tried to draw members from other walks of life. Central Germany was not yet industrialized with an urban proletariat to draw from, but Büchner did manage to include some artisans. Because all its relevant documents, except the *Hessian Messenger*, were later destroyed, little is known of the precise aims of Büchner's group except that it sought to overthrow the Hessian regime through a rebellion that would include the poorest elements of society. In all probability Büchner envisioned a total social and economic revolution, and not merely, as did nearly all German revolutionists of his time, the political liberalization of existing regimes.

Soon after the society had been founded Büchner joined forces with a nearby revolutionary, a pastor named Friedrich Ludwig Weidig, who had been leading agitations in the area for several years. Weidig, more than twice Büchner's age, was fundamentally different from him in aims and temperament. Büchner was economically oriented above all, but Weidig, whose ideas were rooted in Christianity and German idealistic thought, was essentially a democratic liberal with strong leanings toward German national unity. Whatever their differences. Büchner and Weidig banded together for the society's first significant action—a propaganda campaign to arouse the peasants from their customary lethargy. The result was the *Hessian Messenger,* which was to be distributed throughout the local villages and, hopefully, would plant the seeds of later rebellion. The motto which Büchner attached to the pamphlet—"Peace to the huts! War on the palaces!"—gives some indication of its tone. The *Messenger* can be described as a kind of primitive *Communist Manifesto,* certainly more provincial and naive than Marx and Engels' later tract, yet equally impassioned in tone and, like the *Manifesto,* composed of social observation mixed with inflammatory rhetoric. Büchner wrote the first draft of the *Messenger,* but Weidig rewrote it and, to Büchner's great dismay, toned it down considerably. The differences between the two men can be seen, for instance, in the fact that Weidig not only added a number of passages full of Biblical allusions, but that, whereas Büchner had referred to the peasants' enemies as "the rich," Weidig consistently changed Büchner's term to read "aristocrats." The revised version of the pamphlet was printed in July, 1834, and copies were distributed to members of the society, who were then to take them to the various villages. Distribution had scarcely begun, however, when the Hessian authorities were informed of the plot by one of Weidig's former associates. A student friend of Büchner's was caught with copies in his possession and Büchner immediately left Giessen to warn fellow members in other towns. Soon after, Büchner returned to Giessen to find that his lodgings had been searched. The police found no incriminating evidence, and Büchner, trying to evade further suspicion, complained self-righteously to the authorities of the behavior of the police. The authorities, whose information on the plot was probably limited, took some time before making further arrests.

Büchner did not resume his courses at the university, but returned to the home of his parents, who, though aware of the suspicion he was under, knew nothing of his actual activities. His father's political sentiments were by no means radical enough for him to have approved of these activities; moreover, his chief concern at this point was to see his son firmly established in a career. So Büchner spent several uneasy months at home, confiding only in his brother Wilhelm. He knew he would have to flee, but he was also aware that once he did so he could not count on financial support from his parents. In a desperate move to earn money quickly he determined to write a play. During a five- or six-week period in January and early February, 1835, he feverishly composed *Danton's Death*, using as his sources some histories of the Revolution which he found in the family home and others borrowed from the Darmstadt library. He kept a ladder next to the garden wall in order to flee in case the police came to the door. At one point he was summoned before the Darmstadt authorities to answer questions, but sent Wilhelm in his stead; the judge, who knew the Büchner family, apparently did not press charges. As soon as the play was finished Büchner mailed it to Karl Gutzkow, who, though only two years his senior, was already well-known as a writer and as leader of the Young Germany group. Gutzkow was favorably impressed with the play and immediately found him a publisher, but his reply to Büchner's statement of his financial desperation expressed astonishment that Büchner would seek so unlucrative a monetary source as writing a play. In any event, Gutzkow was able to secure him a small sum, though Büchner had fled to Strasbourg in early March, even before the money arrived. His flight was timely, for the police soon after issued a warrant for his arrest. His fellow conspirators were arrested one by one and sentenced to lengthy terms; Weidig committed suicide in prison, and the others were released after some years, many of them emigrating eventually to other countries.

Büchner's flight marked the end of his revolutionary career. Although he was obviously disillusioned, he did not lose hope in eventual social change. His disillusionment proceeded rather from his recognition that Germany was not yet ripe for revolution and that, moreover, the radical opposition existing in Germany was not sufficiently aware of the far-reaching economic changes that would have to accompany the political changes with which they were exclusively concerned. Frustrated in his attempt to be a revolutionist, he determined to devote himself to his scientific studies. In a letter written to his family as soon as he had crossed the border, he expressed the opinion that "in science there is still room enough to do something of excellence, and our times are peculiarly suited to grant recognition in this area." [7]

Büchner remained in Strasbourg a year and a half, until his move to Zurich in October, 1836. At first his father, still angry about his flight (he was unaware of the actual danger his son had faced), refused to continue his financial support, though he later relented; Georg's mother and grandmother, however, secretly sent money to Strasbourg. Although reunited with his fiancée and friends, Büchner had little time now for the relatively carefree life he had led during his earlier stay in Strasbourg. To help support himself he completed translations of two recent prose dramas by Victor Hugo, *Lucrèce Borgia* and *Marie Tudor* (for which, however, he expressed his artistic contempt), which Gutzkow arranged to have published late in 1835, soon after the appearance of *Danton's Death.* He gave up the idea of becoming a physician and determined to prepare for an academic career. Until fairly late in his stay he was uncertain whether to teach primarily biology or philosophy and, in fact, prepared two sets of lecture courses with which to launch his career, one in comparative anatomy and the other in the development of German philosophy since Descartes and Spinoza. During the winter of 1835–36 he completed the research for his thesis on the barbel. He read the results of his research in three papers delivered before the Strasbourg Society of Natural History, which honored him by granting him membership in the society and publishing the thesis in the summer of 1836.

Despite all these other activities, Büchner continued work on various literary projects throughout this period. In response to Gutzkow's repeated requests for articles for a new political and literary review he was founding, Büchner apparently prepared some contributions, but these were never submitted and have never been recovered. He worked at *Lenz*, which he apparently also intended to send to Gutzkow, in late 1835 or early 1836. During the latter period he also completed *Leonce and Lena*, written as part of a competition for the "best German comedy" which a German publishing firm was sponsoring; since the manuscript arrived a few days after the July, 1836, deadline, it was returned to him unopened. Evidence from letters suggests that he worked on *Woyzeck* and *Pietro Aretino* while in Strasbourg. There is also evidence that he suffered from the effects of overwork as a result of all these projects. "I shall not grow old," he reportedly told his mother and a sister, who came to Strasbourg to visit him in the summer of 1836.[8] A diary entry of undetermined date supposedly contained the following world-weary statement: "I am tired, very tired. May the Lord give me peace." [9]

In September, 1836, Büchner sent his thesis to the University of Zurich, which promptly awarded him a doctorate without demanding an oral examination. As a result of this degree he was able to obtain admission to Switzerland. He had long since decided to establish his career in that country, which was doubtless the safest asylum on the European continent for political exiles at that time. Moreover, the University of Zurich, which was only three years old, had attracted to its faculty the most eminent German biologist of his time, Lorenz Oken, who had also had his political troubles in Germany. Throughout his stay in Strasbourg Büchner had feared the possibility of extradition to Hesse and, indeed, had delayed his application for asylum in Switzerland only because the German states had put special pressure on Switzerland early in 1836 to return the refugees who had fled there.

Büchner delivered his trial lecture in Zurich in November and was awarded a lectureship in natural history. He began a course of lectures on the comparative anatomy of fishes and amphibians, lectures which one of his students later remembered for their clarity and concreteness and, above all, for the colorfulness of Büchner's laboratory demonstrations. During the barely four months which he spent in Zurich he led a relatively retiring life, seeing only a number of German exiles, most frequently among them a married couple, Wilhelm and Caroline Schulz, whom he had come to know as fellow refugees in Strasbourg. Shortly before the start of his fatal illness he wrote his fiancée that within a week he should be able to allow three plays to be submitted—"*Leonce and Lena* and two other plays," as he puts it,[10] the other two presumably being *Woyzeck* and *Pietro Aretino*.

Meanwhile, some cases of typhus had broken out in Zurich, and Büchner became a victim. His illness, which set in on February 2, 1837, was recorded in detail by Caroline Schulz, who remained in constant attendance at his bedside. Her diary describes the various fears which he voiced in his delirium and includes the following statement, which he made at the height of his illness and which has sometimes been used to provide a Christian interpretation of *Woyzeck:* "We do not suffer too much pain, indeed we suffer too little, for through our pain we are brought nearer to God." [11] Büchner's fiancée arrived from Strasbourg barely in time for him to recognize her. He died two days later, on February 19.

Büchner had been in Zurich for so short a time that, according to a Strasbourg friend who visited the University later that year, he was soon forgotten by his colleagues. His scientific work, which was influenced by Oken and Goethe and was rooted, to a certain degree, in German idealist preconceptions, was soon rendered obsolete by subsequent research. His literary work, too, seemed destined for obscurity. Gutzkow attempted briefly to keep his name alive through a powerful eulogy published a few months after Büchner's death and through publication, during the next two years, of *Lenz* and a portion of *Leonce and Lena* in a periodical he was editing. Within a short time, however, Büchner's work was quietly forgotten.

iii

Since Büchner died before he could become a man of letters—if, indeed, he ever intended to assume such a role—and since his diary and most of his letters were destroyed or lost, far less is known of his life than of the corresponding years of say, Goethe or Rilke. And it seems a wonder anything has survived at all of his literary remains. Gutzkow, who was Büchner's single contact in the literary world (though the two never met), hoped to publish a collected edition, but was discouraged by Büchner's family, who assigned the task to one of Georg's former schoolmates. The latter failed to carry it out, and an edition was finally published in 1850 by Georg's younger brother Ludwig, who was later to become famed in the Western world for his defense of biological materialism, *Matter and Energy* (1855). Ludwig Büchner's edition was notable for printing some of the letters plus the whole of *Leonce and Lena* for the first time; *Woyzeck*, however, was too difficult to decipher and was omitted. In the following decade Büchner's unpublished letters, together with other papers, perished in a fire in the Büchner home. Büchner's fiancée, in turn, destroyed all the papers that were in her possession before she died, a spinster, in 1880. She is thought to have had Büchner's diary and most of the letters he had written to her. For a long time scholars thought she had destroyed *Pietro Aretino* as well, but there is a good possibility that this play was lost in the fire in the Büchner home.[12]

In the 1870's a young Viennese, Karl Emil Franzos, who recognized the quality of Büchner's writing, set to work tracking down manuscripts as well as personal accounts from those of Büchner's friends who still survived. He found the *Woyzeck* manuscript in the family home and deciphered it as best he could, though it had deteriorated almost to the point of illegibility. He published his version in a journal in 1875 and included it in his famous edition of Büchner's works in 1879. Unfortunately, his somewhat tactless attempt to persuade the aged Minna Jaeglé that it was her "moral duty" to give up the papers she owned resulted in an abrupt refusal.[13]

Although Franzos' edition made possible the revival of interest in Büchner, it was not until two much later editions, that of *Woyzeck*, by Georg Witkowski (1920) and a collected edition by Fritz Bergemann (1922), that Büchner's writings were edited with what we would today consider scholarly responsibility. Few writings from so recent a century have posed such grave editorial problems. Even *Danton's Death*, the one work which appeared in Büchner's lifetime, was heavily bowdlerized in its first edition and its final manuscript lost. Present editions are based largely on two annotated copies of the book which Büchner sent to friends (the annotations, one might add, differ considerably in the two copies). A crucial emendation in the last words of *Leonce and Lena*—the phrase "a coming religion" was changed to "a cosy religion"—was made as late as 1940. It is still uncertain to what degree *Lenz* remains a fragment: did Büchner merely leave out a section in the middle, or did he also intend to go on past the last words? *Woyzeck*, of course, poses the most difficult problems of all: not only are the readings of many words uncertain, but the order of scenes and the exact nature of the ending which Büchner planned have been much disputed.

When Büchner was first discovered in the years following Franzos' edition, his plays were thought to be unstageable. *Leonce and Lena*, the least "experimental" of them, was the first to be produced, in a private performance in Munich in 1885. The first performance of *Danton's Death* took place in Berlin in 1902, though it was not until the development of antirealistic stage techniques in subsequent years that audiences became convinced of its stageworthiness. A performance of *Woyzeck* was not even attempted until the Munich court theater produced it in 1913. Within the next few years the three plays were quickly accepted as classics of the German stage.[14]

As a literary figure, however, Büchner has steadily exerted his influence for the last seventy years. Indeed, each of the diverse personalities who have felt his impact have assimilated different aspects of his work. The major German Naturalist writer, Gerhart Hauptmann, who discovered Büchner in the 1880's, saw him primarily as the portrayer of simple and suffering beings. Frank Wedekind absorbed the grotesque and rebellious elements of his plays, and through Wedekind Büchner came to be one of the spirits presiding over German Expressionism. For the young Bertolt Brecht, Büchner helped provide a language which was earthy and poetic at once. The French *avant garde* dramatists of the 1950's have seen Büchner as a poet of existential anguish and absurdity. Though unable to find a response in its own time, Büchner's work has become an inextricable part of the history of modern literature.

2 *DANTON'S DEATH:* ANTIRHETORIC AND DRAMATIC FORM

AT FIRST GLANCE *Danton's Death* looks like a kind of chronicle play, which in a series of loosely connected scenes details the salient moments of Danton's last weeks, while at the same time providing a good bit of the grim local color appropriate to the period in which it is set. The subtitle which its first publisher (quite to the author's chagrin) attached to it—"Dramatic Images from France's Reign of Terror"—gives some indication of how its early readers, what few there were, must have looked at it. At best it was a drama to be read silently, as one would read narrative history. For an audience accustomed to an essentially Aristotelian concept of the drama—and one for whom Schiller's later plays seemed the highest point that the German serious theater had yet attained—this work could scarcely be considered a drama in any usual sense. In contrast to works such as Schiller's *Wallenstein, Mary Stuart,* and *The Maid of Orleans, Danton's Death* does not present a hero actively, earnestly wrestling with his fate. Nor can we discern a single, closely controlled line of plot development to which all the elements of the drama—the characters, the philosophical matter, the local color—must be rigorously subordinated. From an Aristotelian point of view *Danton's Death* is sprawling and hopelessly uneconomical. The story of Danton's fate is constantly interrupted by seemingly irrelevant genre scenes. Though a certain line of plot can be made out from the more obvious events of the hero's story, the central emotional crises of the play—if we can even call them that—are not, as in an Aristotelian drama, released through the contrivances of plot structure. Characters such as the prostitute Marion are developed in detail only to be dropped immediately after their first appearance. Lengthy political speeches which are only indirectly related to the hero's fate take up a sizable proportion of pages in the play. The conflict between Danton and Robespierre, which in the first half seems the central action of the play, is quite forgotten once Danton is arrested at the end of Act Two.

Yet Büchner, in this, his first creative effort, developed a mode of dramaturgy as sure and exacting as that of any German writer before him. His essential method, as well as his central themes, are implicit in the first page or two of the play:

> [*Hérault-Séchelles and some ladies at a card table; some way off, Danton on a stool at the feet of Julie*]

DANTON Look at that beautiful double-dealing bitch over there! She knows her stuff—slips her husband the hearts, and calls diamonds to the rest of 'em. You could make anyone fall in love with a lie.

JULIE But, Danton, you believe in me, don't you?

DANTON Why ask that? We don't know much about one another, when it comes down to it. We've got very thick skins, and it's not much good fumbling with our hands, wearing each other away. We're lonely, and that's that.

JULIE But you know me, Danton.

DANTON They do call it knowing. You've got dark eyes, and curly hair, and a good complexion, and you keep saying "Darling Georges." But what goes on behind the scenes, girl? Know one another? Go on, we're too clumsy to feel. We'd have to crack the nut open and drag all the little wriggly thoughts out by their tails.

A LADY [*to Hérault*] What are you up to with your fingers now?

HÉRAULT Nothing much!

A LADY Well, don't do that with your thumbs, it isn't nice!

HÉRAULT It's not without its point, love.

DANTON No, Julie, I love you as I love the grave.

JULIE Oh!

DANTON No, listen! There's peace in the grave, they say, the grave and peace are the same thing. Well then, lying with you, I'm buried, I'm at rest. You lovely grave, your lips are funeral bells, your breasts are a mournful mound, your heart's the coffin.

LADY You lose, Hérault!

HÉRAULT An amorous adventure—one generally does.

LADY So you made love by gestures, like a deaf-mute.

HÉRAULT And why not? They're said to involve less misunderstandings than most.

The first lines seem about as offhanded as those with which any tragic drama opens. For the play has no exposition in the conventional sense: we are not given "background details" about the past lives of the main characters, nor are we prepared in any way for the principal actions that will take place in the drama. There is nothing comparable here to those discussions of a momentous past which we find between prince and *confident* at the start of a Racine play, or in the servants' gossip with which so many Ibsen plays begin. Indeed, the lady whom we see so intent at her card game is never developed further in the play. Her function is an altogether temporary one: her game with Hérault is meant to contrast ironically with the very fundamental matters of life and death which Danton chooses to discuss with his wife. Danton's bittersweet apostrophe about the grave, for instance, is rudely interrupted by the lady's announcement that Hérault has lost at cards. In the space of even this single page Büchner shifts back and forth three times between the two contrasting scenes.

One could speak of a kind of dramatic counterpoint that stands behind Büchner's dramaturgy, just as one speaks of a kind of counterpoint in a scene such as the agricultural fair in *Madame Bovary*, in which two and in a sense three actions, all commenting ironically upon one another, are going on at once.[1] Büchner's manner of shifting contexts from one scene or from one group to another is also reflected from moment to moment in the exchanges of dialogue between his characters. Julie's question, "But, Danton, you believe in me, don't you?" is never answered directly by her husband; instead, he shifts the context, as it were, to another area altogether: how can we even talk of believing in each other, he implies, when human beings cannot really know one another? And when Julie responds, "But you know me, Danton," he refuses to accept her on her own ground, but begins, instead, to examine the various semantic possibilities of "knowing." Danton's very statement about the impossibility of human communication is, in fact, a reflection of Büchner's dramatic method: the characters in this play do not really confront each other directly, nor do they persuade one another, nor do they even substantially develop the "plot" through their conversations with one another. A simple question such as Julie's does not, from the play's point of view, at least, deserve a simple answer; the question serves principally as a means of opening up new perspectives of discussion for Danton, indeed, of asserting the unreliability of ordinary language for getting at the essential truths of life.

This opening passage works in still other ways to reveal the play as a whole. Danton's play on the word *hearts* in his first speech is but the first of innumerable examples of puns that occur throughout this play and *Leonce and Lena.* In fact, the various levels on which we can interpret the word —its reference to the frivolities of card games and faithless women, as well as its ironic reminder, through Julie's reaction, of the possibility of faithfulness and devotion between men and women—anticipate some of the basic human issues which reverberate throughout the play. Büchner's decision to open the play with a scene of card players idling away their time not only provided a significant contrast with the second scene—with its picture of the brute, discontented masses during the Revolution—but it gave him the opportunity to embody one of the play's dominant themes in a concrete image at the start: life, as Danton keeps defining and redefining it throughout the work, is essentially a series of games which we play to pass our time away and to remind us as rarely as possible of the great emptiness that stares at us from behind the surfaces of things. Danton's words about finding peace in the grave introduce the play's most persistent single image, or group of images: for sleep and death are most desirable alternatives to life as Danton conceives it, and he invokes them in a multitude of metaphorical combinations in the course of the drama.

ii

The despair that Danton voices at the difficulty of communication points to one of the central insights that govern the composition of the play: for Büchner the mode of language which a character speaks is intimately related to his whole attitude toward life. The play's more talkative characters can be divided into two groups—those, like Robespierre, St. Just, and the stage-prompter Simon, who, in one way or another, still display a confidence in communicating with the world around them, and those, like Danton and his friends, or the prostitute Marion, who have given up hope in the effectiveness of human action and are thus gloomy about the meaningfulness of communication between people. The characters within the first group generally speak a kind of "set" rhetoric, a rhetoric which, one might say, serves as a sign of their commitment to a fairly rigid system of values. As a recent critic of Büchner has shown, the language used by the drunken Simon in accusing his wife of corrupting their daughter sounds uncomfortably similar to the highly emotive rhetoric often found in the German Classical drama, especially in Schiller.[2] When Simon screams, "And having stripped you naked, I shall fling / Your reeking carcass to the dunghill curs," Büchner is not merely parodying the bombast in which Schiller's characters often engage, but he launches into blank verse, which his readers would immediately associate with the heroic world of Classical drama. When Simon starts ranting, "Ah, Lucretia! A knife, give me a knife, my countrymen! Appius Claudius, ah!" he attempts to dignify his personal situation by alluding to ancient myth, but unhappily manages to undercut the rhetorical effect by getting the stories of Lucretia and Virginia mixed up.

In parodying the language of an earlier dramatic style, as he does through Simon's speeches, Büchner is using a technique familiar enough in the history of drama, as in Aristophanes' presentation of Aeschylean bombast in *The Frogs*, or Shakespeare's of the old revenge-play fustian in the player's speech about Hecuba in *Hamlet*. But the language which he gives to Robespierre can scarcely be called parody. For Robespierre is a character whom Büchner treats with total seriousness; he is, after all, Danton's chief antagonist (if one may apply such terms from traditional dramatic criticism to so untraditional a play), and through the tone and length of his speeches Büchner is able to portray a world that seems the total antithesis of Danton's. Yet Robespierre's language, by means of this very tone, suggests the grounds on which we must reject the character who speaks it: "Certain people are saying, 'Pardon the Royalists. Pardon for evil spirits? No! Pardon for innocence, for weakness, for misfortune, pardon for humanity! Only a peace-loving citizen has a right to the protection of society. And only republicans can be citizens of a republic—Royalists and foreigners are enemies."

Like Flaubert and Joyce after him, Büchner defines and evaluates even those characters whom he takes most seriously through their sins of language, without needing to add his comments through their actions or through other characters. The modern reader of course recognizes the now familiar language of totalitarianism in Robespierre's lines. An early nineteenth-century reader would doubtless have recognized the language as Robespierre's even if it had been quoted out of context. And, indeed, the language *is* Robespierre's and not Büchner's at all: by far the greater portion of Robespierre's public speeches in the play is quoted directly (though somewhat rearranged) from the various histories of the French Revolution which Büchner was using.[3] Büchner, who, soon after completing the play, described his task as dramatic poet "to approach as nearly as possible to history as it actually happened,"[4] had no need to invent a language with which to characterize Robespierre; the language was ready-made for him in his sources. The passage quoted above is all Robespierre's except for minor changes in one or two words (changes which do not even come through in the translation I am using). If we compare it to any of the lines spoken by Danton in the play, we quickly note the difference between a sensitive, subtle, much-too-inquiring mind such as Danton's and one which can apprehend reality only in black-and-white terms. Robespierre's language, with its absolute assertions, has a heavy, cliché-ridden deadness about it: only a peace-loving citizen [and no one else] has a right to the protection of society; only republicans [and no others] can be citizens of a republic; Royalists and foreigners [by which he easily disposes of all those who do not fit his definition of republicans] are enemies. Quite in contrast to Danton, who is unable to answer a question directly but must subject it to endless analysis, Robespierre possesses a total, if also a somewhat naive, certainty about the nature of truth: things are either true or false, as his value system chooses to call them; truth does not admit degrees or shades of meaning. The sentences quoted above are tied to one another by a closely contrived dialectic, a dialectic which can jump boldly from premise to conclusion without having to scruple about the validity of either premises or the argumentative process which binds them together. Throughout the play Robespierre's speeches are dominated by abstractions: *virtue, immorality, terror, innocence, the healthy strength of the people* (*gesunde Volkskraft*), to cite some of the most conspicuous examples.

It is significant that Büchner chooses to present Robespierre largely in his public, speech-making role. By far the greater part of his words are spoken as orations, in three successive speeches, first, to an unruly mob in the second scene of the play, next before the Jacobin Club, and then before the National Convention. In each instance his efforts at persuasion are successful (his very success implies Büchner's attitude toward the groups he has managed to convince). But even when he faces Danton alone, he speaks the same language he had spoken on the rostrum: "Vice must receive its punishment, morality must rule by fear." At only one moment in the play can we discern another Robespierre—when Danton, after working to strip his pretensions bare, has left him alone in his room. The Robespierre we see at this point, if ever so briefly, is a man plagued by nightmarish fears, one who, for an instant at least, speaks a dimly poetic language totally devoid of the false clarity that characterizes his more public utterances: "Night snoring over the earth, turning and turning with ugly dreams. All those things taking shape now, and crawling into the house of sleep—unconscious thoughts and desires." By letting his public, rhetorical self master him so fully, he has become, temporarily, a totally opposite self—irrational, confused, the prey of fleeting impressions. And it is in this scene, and here only, that he comes to share a central insight shared also by Danton and his friends—the knowledge of his essential loneliness in a hostile universe. "Camille! They are all going from me," he reflects, directly after his decision to arrest the Dantonists; "everything is empty and waste. I am quite alone."

In Robespierre Büchner has chosen to give us at least a glimpse of a suffering, introspective self that stands behind the hardened public self. In St. Just, however, he presents an unrelentingly rhetorical being who shows no trace of any private self. St. Just is defined by the language he speaks in public, and by nothing more. His long oration before the Convention, which directly follows Robespierre's, attempts to lift the latter's arguments into a cosmic perspective:

> I have noticed that some people in this assembly have remarkably sensitive ears. They don't like any mention of the word "blood." I think a few general observations should be enough to convince them that we are no more cruel in our methods than Nature herself; or, indeed, Time. Nature proceeds in accordance with her own laws, quietly and irresistibly; and every time Man comes into conflict with her, he loses, just like that, he is annihilated.

Robespierre's arguments, however abstract his language, had been limited largely to practical politics—to the business of national security, of discerning friends from foes of the state. St. Just's speech seeks a far loftier level of expression: the laws of Nature must be evoked to justify the arrest of Danton and his friends. Büchner drew only a small bit of this speech from his sources; the sources, in fact, indicate that his actual speech on this occasion was probably not much different from Robespierre's. But Büchner, in creating this speech for St. Just, must have felt the necessity of representing still another mode of rhetoric in his play. The idealism it purports to voice about human progress—"The human race is going to rise from the cauldron of blood, as the earth did once from the waters of sin, rise with mighty strength in its limbs"—seems almost a parody of those lofty expressions about human progress and freedom that mark the dramatic high point of so many German Classical plays: one thinks, for instance, of such tragic figures as Goethe's Egmont, envisioning—with appropriate background music—the benign future which will result from his martyrdom, or of the condemned Marquis Posa, in Schiller's *Don Carlos,* solemnly reminding the hero of that play of the great tasks he must fulfill for the progress of mankind. When seen in the light of such classical moments, the long political speeches in *Danton's Death* seem to voice a hard and bitter skepticism, on Büchner's part, of the validity of rhetoric in voicing any human ideals. "He would rather be guillotined" than make a speech, a character says of Danton at one point; one feels that Danton's attitude toward speech-making is an attitude which stands behind the drama as a whole.

In obvious contrast to the rhetoric of Robespierre and St. Just is the antirhetoric of characters such as Danton and Marion. Marion's lengthy recital of her history is expressed in simple, natural language that stands at an opposite extreme from the play's political dialectic:

> My mother was a very wise woman, she always used to say [it's a virtue] to be pure. When visitors came and started talking about certain things, she used to tell me to leave the room; and if I asked her what they'd meant, she'd say I ought to be ashamed of myself. When she gave me a book to read, there were always some bits I wasn't to look at. I

> was allowed to read the Bible anywhere I liked, because it was all supposed to be holy, you see; but I came across things there that I didn't understand, and I couldn't ask anyone about them, so I kept it to myself, and it worried me.

The utter naturalness with which she speaks may not seem extraordinary to the mid-twentieth-century reader, for whom such a mode of speech might well read like a mere literary convention. But a recitation of this sort is something unique in a serious historical drama written in the 1830's. Though Marion has no effect on the plot (in the conventional sense of that term), her speech has an essential dramatic function—a function which becomes clear, I think, if we compare it to Robespierre's speech to the Jacobins, which occurs only two pages before in the text. In striking contrast to Robespierre's inflated arguments and abstractions, Marion's story consists largely of a series of sense impressions, made without comment on her part. Her sentences are built out of simple clauses, usually connected by *and*, without causal connections. When she describes her emotions she states them directly, as though they were simple facts ("and it worried me"). Her reference, at the beginning, to her mother's admonition of virtue ironically echoes the word *virtue* (*Tugend*) which had resounded three times in Robespierre's speech. She gains the reader's immediate sympathy, but she is never sentimentalized (it is worth noting that by Büchner's time the sympathetically treated prostitute—who goes back at least to Prévost's Manon Lescaut—had long been a stock character in literature). Our sympathy toward her does not derive from the lowliness of her situation, but from the fact that she speaks to us so directly and unpretentiously as a human being.[5] When she describes the differences between her world and that of ordinary people, Büchner resists the temptation to sentimentalize as surely as any serious modern writer since Hemingway would have done: "Other people have Sundays and weekdays, they work six days and pray on the seventh; they get sentimental every time a birthday comes round, and every twelve months they start thinking about the New Year. That's nonsense to me. I don't ever have a day off, and I don't ever change, I stay as I am."

Marion speaks her lines seated on the floor at Danton's feet. From the nature of her speech one can well imagine that she does not even look at him while she talks: like the other "antirhetorical" characters in the play, she speaks what is essentially a monologue, directed less to her listener than to herself or, for that matter, to no one at all. Her unpretentious acceptance of the isolation imposed by her nature and her role in society is reflected dramatically in the isolation which the monologue form suggests. "It was how I was made, that's all, there wasn't anything I could do about it"—thus, without either guilt or pride, she explains her first sexual encounters.

Danton, too, puts special emphasis on the fact that he has remained true to himself, most conspicuously perhaps when he tries to lay bare Robespierre's pretentions of virtue. "Everyone behaves according to his nature, that's to say, he does what's good for *him*," he tells Robespierre after the latter has solemnly asked him, "Have you no respect for morality?" A character such as Robespierre, who refuses to admit the personal needs that motivate all his thoughts and actions, is forced to adopt an inflated rhetoric to justify these thoughts and actions to others and to himself. Characters such as Danton and Marion, in conscious acceptance of their natures, have no need of pretensions, and the language they speak is consequently free of false mannerisms. Danton, of course, speaks a language quite different from Marion's. He is an infinitely more complex character, indeed, one of the most many-sided characters in dramatic literature. Like Hamlet, to whom he has often been compared,[6] one of his functions throughout the play is to subject the assumptions of the other characters to analysis and irony. In the opening scene, he counters even the relatively simple questions of his wife ("But you know me, Danton") with a hard-headed, though also well-meaning, analysis of their verbal content. Although the life he leads is an essentially Epicurean one, he is impatient with those who make a fetish of their Epicureanism. His friend Camille Desmoulins at one point waxes eloquent about the new republic which he envisions replacing the reign of Robespierre ("What we want is naked gods, and easy goddesses, Olympian delights and lovely lips singing of love"); but when he calls on Danton to help bring the new reign into being ("Danton, you must lead the attack at the next Convention!"), Danton mocks his words by turning Camille's command into a schoolboy's grammatical exercise: "I must, you must, he must." Epicureanism, like every other way of thinking, has its own form of rhetoric, and Danton is unwilling to fall into the traps imposed by any such form.

But Danton is surely no devil's advocate, no gadfly indiscriminately running about deflating the pretensions of others. Beneath his manner there lies a profoundly held set of convictions—convictions about the uselessness of ambition and endeavor, disillusionment about the Revolution, a sense of the utter absurdity of all human postures and relationships. What separates Danton from most of the other characters is the *way* in which he holds and voices his convictions. For Danton's convictions do not take the form of dogma or ideology. When he voices them, he does so offhandedly, often jokingly. "I have no hopes of death," he says in one of the prison scenes; "it's a simple form of corruption, whereas life's a more complicated, highly organized kind—that's the only difference between them."

Danton seems so convincing a character for the modern reader through the *tone* with which he speaks. One need only compare him to the character Thomas Payne, who, at the opening of the third act, expounds views not much different from Danton's own.[7] Payne goes to great lengths to demonstrate the nonexistence of God and assert the reality of suffering: like Danton, he makes a point of his hedonism, of "behaving in accordance with my nature." But Payne, though generally a sympathetic character in the one scene in which he appears, expresses his views as a dogmatist, passionately and earnestly; indeed, the portrait we have of him in the play corresponds well with our conception of a man of the Enlightenment: "God does not exist, *because:* either God did or did not create the world. If He did not, then the world is its own first principle, and God does not exist, because God can only be God if He is the principle of all existence. Now we can proceed to prove that God did not create the world."

Danton is beyond such argument. In fact, when Danton and his friends are brought into prison in the middle of Payne's Spinozistic disquisition the atmosphere suddenly changes from one of solemnity to one of joking, though of an obviously macabre kind:

HÉRAULT Good morning, Danton! I ought to say good night. I can't ask how you slept—how are you going to?
DANTON Oh, splendidly, I shall go to bed laughing.

There is nothing of course lightheaded about Danton's attitude: it is the only stance which, given his insights into the nature of things, he can take toward an otherwise unbearable reality. Payne finds consolation by asserting a metaphysic, though a materialistic one, to be sure. Danton, though he declares himself an atheist at one point, can take no metaphysic seriously; his mode of thought undercuts all metaphysics.

In writing of Samuel Beckett, Frederick J. Hoffman makes the generalization that "the philosophical ground of twentieth-century literature has shifted from metaphysics to epistemology. Characters who were formerly maneuvered within an accepted frame of extraliterary reference are now represented as seeking their own definitions and their own languages." [8] It is precisely in this respect that Büchner, specifically through his character Danton, strikes us as so contemporary. Characters such as Robespierre and Tom Payne assert their views with full and unquestioning metaphysical certainty; through the point of view which Danton provides, these certainties are continually undercut by being placed within an epistemological framework. In one instance after another, as we have seen, Danton insists on breaking down language to its empirical foundations—in the skepticism with which he treats his wife's use of the word *knowing,* in the way he systematically picks up and twists around some of Robespierre's most cherished terms —*conscience, virtue, innocence*—even in his habit of punning, which by its very nature implies a skepticism toward the ability of words to reflect and define a stable reality. The stale rhetoric which certain characters in the play speak is a sign of their all-too-naive confidence in fixed ways of thought. Danton's antirhetoric is Büchner's way of demonstrating the falseness of this confidence, and, more fundamentally, of laying bare a world of uncertainties which it is the burden of the play to express so poignantly.

iii

A definition of Büchner's mode of dramaturgy in *Danton's Death* must first take into account his conscious deviations from more conventional forms of drama. At the beginning of the second act, when Camille warns Danton to flee—"Come on, Danton, we haven't got any time to waste"—one would ordinarily expect Danton (if, that is, he were a more traditional sort of tragic hero) either to pick up his coat and leave town before the police arrive, or at least to launch into a solemn statement of his fears, or his regret at leaving. Danton, of course, does no such thing, but instead twists Camille's words around, then loses himself in reflections which have nothing directly to do with the emergency at hand: "But now doth Time waste us. It's remarkably boring, isn't it, always putting your shirt on first and then pulling your breeches up, crawling into bed at night and out again next morning, and placing one foot neatly in front of the other . . . God, it's depressing."

Camille's reply, "You talk like a child," attempts to take us back to the central line of plot, or rather what would seem to be the line of plot. But Danton, just as he confounds the conventional ways of thought of the other characters, also confounds our notions of how a dramatic plot should be developed. One could look at the play as having two lines of action. The first, consisting of Robespierre's actions against Danton and his friends, follows a fairly conventional series of events in political drama: it runs the usual gamut from the initial accusations against a dangerous element within the state through the decision to eliminate the opposition, and the subsequent arrest, trial, appeal, and execution. The second line of action, which consists of the Dantonists' resistance to Robespierre, could better be called a line of inaction, or antiplot. Indeed, there is no real resistance: the progress of the Danton plot consists largely of Danton's quite irrelevant reactions to what is happening to him. Occasionally, as in Camille's lines quoted above, we sense the possibility that the antiplot might tie itself to the Robespierre plot, that Danton might conceivably rise up to a cops-and-robbers game with his opponents. But Danton quickly frustrates any such expectations; his very refusal to resist is Büchner's way of asserting the meaninglessness of the sort of actions we usually associate with dramatic plots.

Not that the horrors of Robespierre's reign are to be interpreted as meaningless. These horrors are painted in very real dramatic terms; but Danton's insights into the nature of things create a perspective so foreign to the one in which the Robespierre plot takes place that he is rendered incapable of coping with these horrors in any effective way. The more conventional tragic hero at least makes an attempt to be "effective," and much of the conventional tragic catharsis results from our admiration at his attempts to act in the face of overwhelming odds. But Danton remains passive and ineffectual from the beginning, at least in terms of the Robespierre plot. In his pioneering study of Büchner, Karl Viëtor has called Danton the first truly passive hero in German drama.[9] Through this passivity, which he betrays in his early speeches, we should be warned from the start not to look at the play in any of the usual Aristotelian ways. Thus, we cannot expect the hero at the end to experience a sudden grand moment of recognition. Danton pronounces essentially the same insights about the burdens of mortality at the beginning of the play as at the end; unlike an Oedipus or a Lear, he is never shown in an initial state of "innocence" from which, as a result of the play's action, he enters the world of "experience." He does not have to wrestle with his fate in order to become aware of the uselessness of action; he is aware of it from the start and, in fact, would prefer to have his fate over with as soon as possible. The increasing anguish of the play resides in the way he must bide his time for so long in full knowledge of what awaits him.

If the larger structure of the play can be defined through the juxtaposition of plot and antiplot, Büchner's mode of composition from moment to moment can be described through his alternation of contrasting scenes. As a very obvious instance, the first scene, with its bored dandies idling away their time with games, contrasts markedly with the second scene, which vividly depicts the discontented mob sweeping through the streets. Moreover, the introspection in which Danton engages so subtly in the first scene finds its opposite in the harsh rhetoric with which Robespierre quiets the crowd in the second. In the last two acts the series of poignant scenes of the Dantonists in prison alternate with scenes of dissident groups in the streets, of St. Just and his committee outdoing one another in exhibiting their talents at callousness, of carters making macabre jokes while waiting to pick up the next batch of victims for the guillotine. Julie's decision to join her husband in death is set next to a scene in which Citizen Dumas self-righteously defends sending his wife to the guillotine.

The play of contrasts is not confined to the relationships between scenes, but is inherent in the internal organization of individual scenes. In discussing the opening scene, I noted the sustained contrast between the card-game conversation of Hérault and his partner and the more fundamental matters being discussed by Danton and his wife; in a similar way, the solemnity of the Tom Payne scene is contrasted with the joking between Danton and his friends as they are being led into prison. The most obvious function of Büchner's technique is that it enables him to comment ironically on the action without having to introduce characters to argue his own point of view to the reader. To put it another way, the method allows him to treat such seemingly negative characters as Robespierre and St. Just with a high degree of objectivity, even sympathy. St. Just, for instance, though my description may have made him seem direly villainous, would not strike an audience as an ordinary stage Machiavel; indeed, hearing his great oration, one might well feel momentarily persuaded by its resounding arguments. The air of objectivity which Büchner achieves is perhaps the dramatic equivalent of the kind of objectivity which novelists in the Flaubertian tradition were later to seek. By suppressing authorial commentary these novelists developed certain devices similar to Büchner's—ironic juxtapositions, the depiction of a character through the clichés in which he speaks and thinks—to enforce their meanings. And, like many modern novelists, Büchner places much of the burden of interpretation on the spectator. In what seems to me the most penetrating essay on the play yet to appear in English, Lee Baxandall attempts to describe the spectator's role:

> What in fact happens here, in this seemingly passive, fragmented, lyrical and monologic play, is that the *spectator* has become the genuine "hero." Situated superior to the events which transpire on the stage, the spectator reflects and makes observations and formulations of what he sees, and he draws conclusions which transcend the knowledge of any of the characters. Deprived of classicism's easy-to-follow causal plot line, and deprived of classicism's summarizing declarations, the spectator assumes the burden of making decisions, a burden formerly reserved to the dramatic hero.[10]

I am none too sure that Danton himself is quite so neutral a hero as Baxandall implies: certainly Danton's comments on the other characters are meant to be taken quite seriously. Yet Danton too is subjected to criticism through Büchner's use of ironic contrasts: when Robespierre succeeds in quieting the crowd in the second scene, Danton's introspections, which had seemed so wise in the first scene, suddenly impress us with their ineffectualness.

To speak of ironic contrasts at the basis of Büchner's technique is perhaps to suggest too much; the word *con-*

trasts implies opposites, as though each scene reversed the tone and meaning of the preceding one. It would be more accurate to describe Büchner's technique as one of continually shifting perspectives. Just as our perspective upon Danton in the first scene is altered by our view of the street crowds and Robespierre's speech, so our perspective on Robespierre is altered by Marion's speech, with its ironic echo of his favorite word, *virtue;* the word, indeed, reechoes at various moments in the play, each time creating a somewhat different perspective on Robespierre and his world.

The composition of individual scenes is marked not only by the sharp contrasts I have described, but by frequent, subtle changes of tone. The last of the scenes in the Conciergerie (Act IV, Scene 5), which records the prisoners' last moments together before they are carted through the streets to the guillotine, moves gradually through a series of moods—from the grim punning of the opening:

DANTON You know what we'll be soon?
FABRE No.
DANTON What you spent all your life making—*des vers,*

through a number of questions in which the prisoners translate their fears into universal terms reminiscent of the most agonized moments of *King Lear:*

HÉRAULT Are we poor little suckling pigs for a lordly table, thrashed to death to make us tastier?
DANTON Are we children, put into the world to be roasted in the red-hot arms of Moloch, and tickled with beams of light to amuse the gods with our crowing?
CAMILLE And is the ether with its gold eyes a dish of golden carp, laid on the roaring dinner table of Olympus, with the gods always merry, and we poor fish dying?

while the scene is finally resolved on a serene note:

HÉRAULT Cheer up, Camille, we've got a lovely night for it. It's quite still, and look at the clouds—like a dying Olympus over France, with the shapes of gods fading and sinking away.

In other scenes the perspective shifts rapidly from moment to moment, most memorably perhaps in the promenade scene (Act II, Scene 2), in which Danton and Camille walk through the streets observing a multitude of little scenes—a whore and a soldier bantering with one another, an elegant lady, with her daughter, spouting polite platitudes, two gentlemen in absurd snatches of meaningless conversation—all woven together into a closely worked fabric.

By refusing to follow the classical pattern of plot development, in which every element would be subordinated to the central dramatic line, Büchner was able to create an expansive and rich texture of persons, atmospheres, and events. Though Danton's fate remains at the center of his vision, Büchner has portrayed the larger historical milieu with a breadth and vigor that still seem remarkable in an age such as ours, which can take for granted the expansive methods of Brechtian epic theater. "The dramatic poet is in my view nothing but a historian," Büchner wrote in a letter defending his use of "vulgarities" in the play, "to whom he is however superior in that he creates history for us a second time; projects us forthwith directly into the life of times past, instead of giving us a dry narrative, and gives us characters instead of characteristics, and actual persons instead of descriptions." [11] The directness and objectivity which he sought were possible only by means of the dramatic method he employed.

Still, despite the sudden contrasts and the constant modulations of tone, *Danton's Death* builds steadily in intensity and, in its final scenes, achieves a climax as moving and, in fact, as terrifying as that of any German drama before or after. The comic and absurd moments that alternate with the more somber ones serve not so much to mitigate the tragic effect, but, rather like the gravedigger scene in *Hamlet*, to increase it. The scene of the joking carters is sandwiched between one of the prison scenes and the passage in which Lucille Desmoulins, already close to madness, comes to speak to her husband through the window of the prison. For the hard-headed modern reader Lucille's agitated lines—"Listen, my darling, people are saying you've got to die, and they're making awful faces about it. You, die! I can't help laughing at the silly faces"—these lines seem moving at this point precisely because Büchner has refused to bully the reader into a somber mood; the comedy, rather than undercutting the tragedy, works to validate it and augment it.

Much of the pathos of the final scenes, moreover, comes from the manner in which Büchner has chosen to develop the two grieving women, Lucille and Julie. Julie's death, in fact, has a formality and solemnity about it reminiscent—at least if we look at it out of context—of death scenes in earlier tragedies (for example, that of Shakespeare's Juliet):

I mustn't keep him waiting, even a moment.
[*She takes out a phial.*]
Come on, little priest, your amen will send me to bed.
[*She goes to the window.*]
It is lovely to say good-bye like this. I've only got to shut the doors behind me—so.

Julie's lines, not only here but throughout the play, show a purity of expression rare in a work whose more sympathetic characters speak with tough-minded irony and whose unsympathetic characters are exposed to us through the naïveté of their rhetoric.

It is significant that Büchner, despite lifting from his sources innumerable lines spoken by Robespierre and Danton, diverged radically from his sources in his treatment of Julie and Lucille: the real Julie (whose name was Sébastienne-Louise) was a girl who had been married to Danton for only six months at the time of his death and who herself was remarried a few years later, while the real Lucille neither went mad nor died voluntarily, but was executed for attempting to free her husband. But both women, as Büchner created them, were necessary to the design of the play, for both, in their various ways, could express a kind of pathos which their much more Stoic-minded husbands could not have voiced so directly. In the last Conciergerie scene the prisoners admit the uselessness of their Stoicism and ask each other why they cannot "bleat or roar or howl just as it takes you"; yet they are never able to release their emotions with the unself-conscious force of an Oedipus or a Lear. Even Lucille is unable to purge her emotions through screaming, though she tries to scream on the streets:

I'll lie down on the ground and scream, so that everything's frightened, and stops, and doesn't go running on any more.

[*She lies down, covers her eyes, and screams. Then, after a pause, she gets up again.*]

It's no use, everything's just as it was—the houses, and streets, and the wind blowing the clouds along. I must bear it, that's all.

The uselessness of Lucille's screaming is emblematic, I think, of Büchner's attitude toward older conceptions of tragedy; yet through his honesty in refusing to let her indulge in the rhetoric of a tragic pose, we feel all the more prepared to assent emotionally to the overwhelmingly tragic facts of the play.

iv

Until relatively recent times *Danton's Death* was looked upon as a primarily political drama, and, in particular, as a kind of apology for the French Revolution. For instance, the German historian Treitschke, writing in the late nineteenth century, took it for granted that the play was essentially a reflection of Büchner's radical doctrines:

> Among all his [Büchner's] contemporaries only Carlyle was able to portray the horrors of those days [the Reign of Terror] with such terrifying truth, but while the Scot passionately expressed his moral disgust at these events, the German, in all seriousness, thought of glorifying the Revolution through a work which can only arouse a feeling of abhorrence. One wonders if this, the most talented writer of the era of Young Germany, might perhaps have been able to outgrow his disconsolate materialism.[12]

If a conservative such as Treitschke could attack the play on political grounds, radicals could, by the same token, praise the doctrines which they thought they discerned in it. In 1886, when it was still little known in German, the play was printed in a German-language edition in America in a series entitled the "Socialistic Library," designed for liberal-minded German immigrants.[13] Some of its early German stage productions, most notably the famous Max Reinhardt version in Berlin in 1916, succeeded in continuing this view of the drama by making the Paris mobs seem the play's hero.[14] The distinguished Marxist critic Georg Lukács would have it that Büchner divided his sympathy between Danton, Robespierre and St. Just, and that in Danton he was attempting to depict an essentially eighteenth-century mind who, in contrast to Robespierre, lacked insight into the nature of the revolutionary process.[15]

All these views of the play, rightist and leftist alike, obviously start from the premise that since Büchner led a revolutionary conspiracy and wrote the inflammatory *Hessian Messenger, ergo* his dramatic work attempted to propound a revolutionary thesis. In the years immediately following the Second World War, Büchner's critics sometimes went to an opposite extreme; looking at the play totally from Danton's point of view, and taking some of the more despairing lines—for instance, Danton's "The world is chaos. Nothingness is the world god yet to be born"—as their prime texts, they often read the play as an essentially nihilist tract.[16] If one must choose between extremes, there is doubtless more truth to the latter interpretation, if only to the extent that Danton's perspective on reality seems more convincing than that of Robespierre or of the crowd. But *Danton's Death*, indeed, all of Büchner's works, stubbornly resist being pigeon-holed into thesis categories: his best German critics of the last few years, moreover, have been at pains to work out the meaning of his plays through detailed analyses of the texts, without preconceptions about any ideologies that might lie beneath them.[17]

Yet I should maintain that *Danton's Death* is a profoundly political drama, though surely not in the old-fashioned sense of the term, which would see such a work as an attempt to propagate a particular political view. Rather, *Danton's Death* is political in another, less easily discernible sense: if I may borrow from Irving Howe's definition of the political novel—a definition based on his readings of works such as *The Charterhouse of Parma, The Possessed, The Princess Casamassima*—the play is political through its attempt "to show the relation between theory and experience, between the ideology that has been preconceived and the tangle of feelings and relationships [the author] is trying to represent." [18] Similarly to the political novels which Howe discusses, *Danton's Death* seeks to demonstrate the tragic gap between political ideals and political actualities, to examine, for instance, the paralyzing effect that the political process can have on men of good will such as Danton and his friends. Although the play has much to say about the nature of personal relationships, it is not primarily a drama of private or social experience in the way that the dramas of Chekhov or Strindberg or Beckett are. In *Danton's Death* the political dimension is always discernible; Danton's private despair, for example, gains meaning precisely because we measure it against the smug certainties and optimistic cant of Robespierre.

It is significant that Büchner chose to set his play in the darkest hour of the Revolution, when the great ideals which had once motivated all his characters were put to their most bitter test. The masses at this point are thoroughly disillusioned and can be kept in tow only through the shrewdest demogogery; the revolutionary leaders can maintain their power only through their systematic annihilation of all conceivable subversion; traditional human relationships—between husband and wife (Danton and Julie, Camille and Lucille), or between life-long friends (Camille and Robespierre had been friends in school)—are threatened at the root. Out of this dramatic image emerge a series of insights into the nature of politics—that ideals, in the face of challenging events, can become hardened into ideology; that the ideology which a man embraces is a consequence of his personal needs, above all, his need to survive;

that, in the light of overpowering and uncontrollable forces, the very need to survive is a questionable value. The political situation which Büchner depicts is inextricably bound up with the personal situations of his characters, as well as with their metaphysical speculations. Through the techniques which Büchner employs—the ironic contrasts, the air of objectivity with each of the characters seems to be created—he rarely needs to insist directly on the connections between the political and the personal realms; he does so only at moments, as when Danton attempts to cut down Robespierre's pretensions to his face—"Everyone behaves according to his nature, that's to say, he does what's good for *him.*" For the most part Büchner lets the play speak for itself; the reader is left to size up Robespierre's pronouncements both on their own rhetorical merits and through the meanings they take on through the context with which they are surrounded.

If we insist on tying the play to the author's biography, we could say it is less Büchner the Revolutionist than Büchner the Scientist who speaks to us in the drama. Indeed, the strong antiteleological bent of Büchner's inaugural lecture in Zurich, above all, his insistence in this lecture that "nature does not exhaust itself through an infinite chain of causes, each determined by the last, but is in all its manifestations sufficient unto itself" [19]—such a statement, though part of a lecture on the cranial nerves, forms a kind of correlative to his dramatic method.

Not that I mean to underestimate the intensity of Büchner's political commitment. But if *Danton's Death* is in certain respects a drama about political disillusionment, one must point out that some of Danton's most despairing lines are echoed by statements that we find in Büchner's letters well before the conspiracy in which he was engaged in 1834. Compare, for instance, these lines written after his meningitis—"O, what miserable, screeching musicians we are! This groaning on our torture-rack, could it be there only that it may pass through the gaps in the clouds and, echoing further and further on its way, die like a breath of melody in celestial ears?" [20] with these lines spoken by Danton in the last scene in the Conciergerie—"But we're the unfortunate musicians performing on our unhappy bodies. Do you mean that the nasty bungling noises they produce are only to float up and die away as a voluptuous breath in these heavenly ears?"

By the same token Büchner's letters after the time of *Danton's Death* show his continued hopes for fundamental changes in the economic and social structure of the German states, though he usually tempers these hopes with skepticism about the immediate means by which these changes might be wrought.[21] Above all, one must not attempt to tie the revolutionary doctrines of the *Hessian Messenger* to those which Büchner attributes to Robespierre and his committee. For one thing, the *Messenger* is a pamphlet directed against tyranny, both economic and political; the revolutionary power at the period he has chosen to set the play has itself become a tyranny of the most uncompromising sort. Moreover, Büchner's prose in the *Messenger* has a concreteness and a liveliness which we never find in the pronouncements of Robespierre and St. Just. The pamphlet is passionate and earthy at once; its very extravagance gives it an appealing quality which we rarely feel in the political rhetoric of the past—

> Go to Darmstadt and see what fine times your lords are having on your money, and then tell your starving wives and children how grandly their bread has been stuffed into the stomachs of strangers, tell them of the fine clothes, dyed in their sweat, and of the elegant ribbons, which are cut from the callouses on their hands, tell them of the stately houses, which are built out of the bones of the common folk; and then go crawl back into your smoky huts.[22]

I have chosen to quote this passage not only because it exemplifies the flavor that pervades the pamphlet as a whole, but because its idea is echoed at one point in *Danton's Death,* in a speech by a citizen in the mob: "Danton's got nice clothes, Danton's got a nice house, Danton's got a nice wife; he has his bath in Burgundy, he eats game off silver dishes, and when he's tight he sleeps with your wives and daughters. He used to be poor like you." The difference in the effect of the two passages could not be greater. The citizen's speech comes directly after Danton has lost his appeal before the tribunal and forcibly been removed from the courtroom. Our sympathies are unquestionably with Danton at this point, especially so because in the course of this single speech the crowd is shown turning against Danton. Büchner, as we can see, was well aware of the differences between the demands imposed by dogma and drama. He underlined his awareness of this difference in a letter written to his family a year after completing the play; denying his adherence to the doctrines of the literary radicals known as Young Germany (doctrines far less extreme, for that matter, than the ones he had advocated in the *Messenger*), he writes: "I go my own way and remain in the field of drama which has nothing to do with all these controversial issues. I draw my characters in accordance with Nature and History and laugh at those who would like to make me responsible for their morality or immorality." [23]

Still, one can discern a particular mode of commitment, social more than political in nature, which thoroughly pervades all Büchner's works. I refer to his stress on the reality of human suffering. One need not wonder that it is possible for an ingenious stage director to portray the Parisian mob in a favorable light. Although it is not hard for a reader to note that Büchner's mob is every bit as unreliable and fickle as Shakespeare's in *Coriolanus*, Büchner presents their grievances with a real, if also hard-headed sympathy.

But suffering is not limited to the crowd; it is shared by characters of all factions, by Robespierre in his monologue after his confrontation with Danton, by Danton and his friends in the Conciergerie. Thomas Payne's line "The least little flicker of pain, if it only involves an atom, is enough to split the creation wide open from top to bottom," symbolizes an attitude and a commitment which underlies Büchner's whole poetic world. This human sympathy which Büchner manifests so all-pervasively is related, I think, to the dramatic sympathy which he grants his characters and which, in turn, underlies his dramatic technique. Robespierre, Danton, Payne, Marion, Lucille, the starving people of Paris—all are fellow sufferers, whatever their mutual antagonisms and differences in personality. "People call me a scoffer," he once wrote in a letter to his family; "it is true, I often laugh at people; yet I don't laugh at *how* someone is a human being, but simply at the fact *that* he is a human being, for which of course he is not to blame, and I often laugh at myself as one who shares his fate." [24] The piety toward his fellow beings which he expresses here is fundamental to his refusal to pass judgment directly on his characters, but rather to present them in all their immediacy, for what they are; it is an attitude, moreover, which more surely shapes his work than any of the doctrines, political or philosophical, which have been applied to interpret it.

v

In contrast to most of the German Classical dramas, *Danton's Death* is in prose, yet in the impression it leaves it is one of the most poetic of German plays. For one thing, it displays a luxuriance of metaphor which German dramatic blank verse had insisted on doing without. Even the abstract Robespierre muses metaphorically to himself in his monologue: "Night snoring over the earth, turning and turning with ugly dreams." Danton's speeches, especially in the prison scenes, not only contain an amazing number of poetic figures, but they also show a complexity of tone and a concentration of language which the rhetorical conventions of German Classical drama normally excluded from dramatic verse. Take the following lines: "I feel as if I were stinking already. Poor old body, I'll hold my nose and pretend you're a nice woman that's got a bit sweaty [and smelly] dancing and be polite to you. My word, body, think of the times we've had together, you and I." Fear of death, courtliness of manner, tender regret about the fleetingness of past pleasures—all are fused together in this image with a characteristically Shakespearean boldness. Moreover, the final Conciergerie scene, in which the prisoners voice their fears in a series of lyrical outbursts, has a grandeur of language which Büchner was never to surpass, for the type of dramatic structure toward which he moved in his remaining works left no opportunity for such displays of eloquence.

Yet *Danton's Death* is surely not poetic in the nineteenth-century sense of the term—its bawdiness and its lack of solemnity would hardly have made such a term suitable—but in a peculiarly modern sense, in the way that we think of works such as Joyce's *Ulysses* or the plays of Bertolt Brecht as poetic. Like these works of our own century, it is able to achieve a poetic effect for us only through its conscious refusal to seem poetic in any traditional way. The ironic contrasts, the bantering of the mob, Danton's jibes at Robespierre's pompousness—all these serve as a kind of guarantee that the drama will not get rhetorically out of hand, that the deeply moving dramatic effects toward which the play is building will be backed up by a tough-minded attitude toward all human experience. The pathos of Lucille's and Julie's final speeches, or of Camille's tender expressions about his wife in the last act, is possible only because of the down-to-earth context which Büchner has built up throughout the play. Danton's *de profundis* cry, "Are we children, put into the world to be roasted in the red-hot arms of Moloch, and tickled with beams of light to amuse the gods with our crowing?" carries such great emotional weight precisely because of the surprise we feel at words like *roasted* and *tickled*, which would seem quite indecorous in more conventionally poetic surroundings. Like innumerable modern writers, Büchner allows himself to release feeling by first assuring his audience, as it were, that he has properly screened the feelings he chooses to display.

In something of the same way he allows Danton to achieve the stature of a hero only by first refusing him the conventional heroic attributes. At first glance, Danton, with his continual complaints of ennui, seems like one of the early examples in drama of the hero as aesthete. The notions he voices—on the meaninglessness of ordinary routine, on the burdens of time, on human loneliness—have much in common with the views of a whole tradition of characters from Werther through J. Alfred Prufrock.[25] Yet Danton maintains a sturdiness and a dignity uncommon among such heroes. We find in him none of Werther's helplessness or self-pity, none of Prufrock's absurdity, nor does he indulge in the self-glorification of Byron's various marked men, or in the over-refined sensibilities of Chekhov's superfluous country gentlemen. What ties him to this tradition of characters, besides some of the generalities on life they express in common, is the fact that he impresses us at first as a consciously conceived anti-hero.

The anti-hero is only possible in a literary tradition which has already represented real heroes—successful men of action such as Goethe's Götz von Berlichingen, or heroes of the mind such as Schiller's Mary Stuart and Joan of Arc, who by dint of will achieve at least an inward victory in the face of inevitable doom. By presenting an anti-hero such as Danton, Büchner implies that such earlier forms of heroism were possible only in a less self-conscious stage of human development; being a hero in Büchner's world means being a bit crude and even ludicrous. The men of action and the men of will in *Danton's Death* are characters such as Robespierre and St. Just. Robespierre's success in getting the crowd under control in the second scene contrasts startlingly with the loquacious passivity which Danton had demonstrated at the opening, yet through Danton's insights into Robespierre's motives (as well as through the crudity of the rhetoric with which the latter exposes himself), Robespierre ultimately seems somewhat naive and absurd in his busy political doings. Danton impresses us throughout as mentally and morally superior to his opponent and thus makes the value of political activity seem at best a questionable one. "I give him rather less than six months before he comes down my way," Danton says of Robespierre just before his execution, and the audience, with its hindsight into subsequent history, sees yet another confirmation of the uselessness of all Robespierre's efforts. (One might note that Danton's prophecy of Robespierre's imminent end was contained in Büchner's sources and was thus no mere contrivance by which he could gain an easy plus-mark for his hero.)

The superiority we see in Danton is earned not only through his exposure of the absurdity of Robespierre and others, but through the honesty with which he views even his own absurdity and that of the whole human condition. Among the many metaphors he chooses to symbolize the absurdity of human action is the ambition of children to be promoted in school: "Start in the first form, and move up to the second, and then the third, and so on? Well, I'm sick of school benches and sitting around all this time like a monkey with a sore backside." It is characteristic that Danton's generalizations about life not only take such metaphorical form, but that he places himself in such absurd postures. He resolutely refuses to assume the more comfortable poses to which his unfortunate fate might well have entitled him. He eschews self-pity, but is honest enough about his fears of death. He is never even tempted by the consolations that accompany martyrdom. The closest he comes to a pose—and this only through his refusal to indulge himself emotionally—is Stoicism; yet even this is seen through and rejected: "Those Stoics gave themselves a good sort of feeling inside, you know. It's not bad fun to pull your toga on and have a quick look round to see what sort of a shadow you're throwing." His only pose, if it is a pose at all, is his joking. His deepest fears are expressed in jokes, his affections toward his friends are conveyed jokingly (though with an underlying seriousness), his last words to the executioner are a joke. To the modern mind joking is perhaps the noblest stance a person can assume in the face of inevitable doom; and Danton, even if he cannot die sword in hand like Hamlet, gains a certain nobility for us through his refusal to assume at least any of the conventional poses.

But Danton's doom is not inevitable at the *start* of the play. By a strange paradox, although the image of the world that we are presented with from the beginning is a hopeless one, it is amply clear that Danton might have avoided death by escaping in time. In contrast to the traditional tragic hero, who comes to see the world as black only when he realizes that his own doom is inevitable, Danton has no illusions about the world from the start and quietly wills his doom. Büchner of course never makes clear to us whether Danton's failure to save himself was a consequence of his world-view or whether his world-view was a rationalization of a psychological paralysis which precluded even the action of escape: such causal explanations could not (and need not) be made within the confines of the dramatic method to which Büchner subjected himself in writing the play. In something of the same way he never makes clear whether Danton expected that his refusal to escape would result in his arrest, or whether he really believed his much repeated statement that the committee would not dare to arrest an old fellow revolutionary like himself. Both sides of this ambiguity are expressed in his words when he enters the prison: "It's good to die of a stroke; who wants it to be 'after a long illness'? And, as a matter of fact, I never thought they'd have the nerve." By leaving both possibilities open (and both possibilities were suggested by Büchner's sources), Büchner is able to maintain our sense of Danton's world-weariness and at the same time to suggest a kind of reckless nonchalance in him.[26]

This nonchalance, combined as it is with an unthinking confidence in his personal security, is the only indication we get in the play of that heroic side of Danton which, two years before, had been able to save the Republic in the face of enemy armies. We are reminded of Danton's past heroism on a number of occasions, but the present Danton generally looks back at his past actions with self-recrimination. As a man of action he had been forced into brutalities—most notably the September Massacres—which, from his present introspective state of mind, haunt him in his sleep with a turbulence reminiscent of the night-thoughts of Lady Macbeth. "You were saying something about sins, and then you cried out 'September'," Julie tells him, trying to shake him out of his self-tormenting trance. But later, before the Revolutionary Tribunal, his accusers treat him with such condescension that his anger is kindled and he displays something of the heroic spirit which he had shown in the past: "On the field of Mars I declared war on the monarchy: on August the tenth I struck it, on January the twenty-first I killed it, and I threw down the royal head as my challenge to all the other kings in the world." Several scenes later, when he presents his appeal to the Tribunal (Act III, Scene 9), he accuses his accusers with all the vehemence (though without the clichés) of a Robespierre or a St. Just; his tirade, indeed, is so powerfully persuasive that the audience rallies to his side and the Tribunal is forced to remove him and his fellow prisoners before they can turn the tide to their cause. Even the anti-hero has his moments of traditional heroism.

If Danton displays a heroic quality that sometimes confounds his anti-heroic pretensions, he also possesses an immense vitality which belies the resignation he professes throughout the play. This vitality is inherent in the language he speaks, in the joking, in the poetic evocation of his fears, in the endless succession of metaphors he contrives to express his resignation. One often, in fact, feels as though his general passivity is compensated for by a corresponding degree of verbal activity. But this vitality of language is not confined to Danton alone, it is something one feels in the play as a whole; the very richness of its poetry gives the play a certain exuberance that almost cancels out the cynicism and despair that seem to emanate from it. Indeed, as Egon Schwarz has suggested, wit functions throughout Büchner's dramas as a kind of alternative to the nihilism which they so often attempt to express.[27] Schwarz cites a passage from *Danton's Death* as characteristic: a young man sporting a handkerchief is accosted by the mob, who scream: "He's got a handkerchief! An aristo! Hang him on the lamppost! The lamppost!" As they are about to string him up, he replies, "I don't see that it's going to improve the light." The mob, surprised by his show of wit, decide to let him go.

Although the wit and the general verbal exuberance suggest at least a possible release from the bleakness of the world which Büchner has created, one must not underestimate the dark power which issues from this world. The central image out of which *Danton's Death* is built is that of an upside-down world, one in which all order has been inverted. Büchner sensed the possibilities of this image in a letter he wrote two years before the play:

> I was studying the history of the Revolution. I felt myself as though utterly crushed under the frightful fatalism of history. I find in the nature of mankind a horrible parity and in human relationships an inexorable force that is given to all and to none. The individual a mere froth on the wave, greatness a mere chance, the dominance of genius a puppet's game, a ridiculous struggling against an iron law, the recognition of which is the highest achievement, but which to control is impossible.[28]

The Reign of Terror, especially in that later stage of it which Büchner chose to depict, provided the perfect scenic embodiment for Danton's notions about the meaninglessness of life. Within this inverted image, all expressions relative to a normal state of things—expressions of affection, petty jealousies, fear of showing bad manners—come to seem hopelessly absurd. "Your hair and nails get in such a state, you feel so filthy," Lacroix complains about his stay in prison, after which Hérault continues the joke: "Do be a bit more careful, you sneezed right in my face!"

Lacroix and Hérault of course are conscious of the absurdity of their remarks, but the less shrewd characters of the play—those not capable of the "high achievement" of recognizing the "iron law" of which Büchner speaks in the letter quoted above—are trapped by their own absurdity whenever they express themselves in normal terms. Take, for instance, the conversation of three women on the street directly after the execution of Danton and his friends:

FIRST WOMAN That Hérault was smashing, wasn't he!

SECOND WOMAN I saw him standing in front of that Arc de Triomphe on Constitution Day, you know, and I said to myself then, I said, "Now there's one that would look nice on the guillotine," yes.

THIRD WOMAN I always say you ought to see a man in different surroundings; I'm all for these public executions, aren't you, love?

Sentiments that would be perfectly acceptable in a normal world—praise for a man's looks, the desire to know what other people are really like—become not only comic and absurd in this abnormal context, but in the light of all that has happened in the play, they achieve a positively chilling effect. Indeed, Büchner's various allusions to a normal world only serve to make the inverted world all the more frightening.

The vision of life that emerges from this collocation of worlds is a profoundly modern one, and but a step or two removed from that of such a modern writer as Kafka. The absurdities out of which Kafka's world is built are obviously far greater in number and intensity than those we find in Büchner. And to achieve his characteristic effects Kafka has had to distort our conceptions of reality to the point where, though we recognize the relation of his world to our everyday world, we are also aware that his world has the essential lineaments of a dream. In Büchner, at least in *Danton's Death,* we are never allowed to feel we are witnessing a dream distortion. The inverted world of the Reign of Terror is presented to us as a mimetic representation of a recognizably real world, with its backgrounds minutely filled in. It is history, after all.

In the final reckoning the only escape from the world of this play is death. Danton made this clear, of course, on the first page of the text, and the play simply goes on to confirm his statement. Of the various ways that the characters in the play go to their death, only Julie's is the kind one is accustomed to find in earlier tragic dramas. Her death has no trace of the absurd about it; she meets it voluntarily, nobly, self-sacrificingly, as though asserting that traditional values still have some meaning. In sharp contrast, Danton and his friends go passively to their death, and in full awareness of its lack of meaning. Unlike such heroes as Goethe's Egmont or Schiller's Joan of Arc they can never tell themselves that they died for any higher cause. The very manner of their execution underscores the meaninglessness of their deaths. "Oh, if only it were a fight, if only it were slashing and hitting. . . . I *won't* be killed by a machine!" Danton cries out in the Conciergerie. In his last words to the executioner, when he speaks of heads accidentally kissing as they fall into the basket, he recognizes the total lack of dignity in such a death.

Had Büchner ended the drama directly after the execution, the effect of the ending would have been similar to the effect of K's death at the end of Kafka's *The Trial:* a passive, meaningless death as a final, none-too-surprising confirmation of the world-view that has been suggested throughout each work. But Büchner chose to work out still another possibility latent within his image of an inverted world; by closing the play with Lucille's death (or, more precisely, her arrest) he was able to give the play a memorably assertive ending that resounded with a series of ironies. I noted earlier that the real-life prototype of Lucille was arrested for far more conventional reasons; but one of Büchner's sources spoke of a number of women who, lacking the courage to take poison, shouted "Long live the king" in full certainty of dying shortly thereafter.[29] Lucille's gesture has the willfulness we associate with many a martyr's death. Yet it is the very opposite of martyrdom: whereas a martyr dies with his most sacred beliefs on his lips, Lucille wills her death by shouting words that mean nothing to her, in fact, words she quite obviously disbelieves in. Moreover, the idea occurs to her quite suddenly, almost as a whim. Her gesture is of course an absurd one, but—quite in contrast to Julie's suicide, which sought to affirm traditional values—it represents the only self-assertive gesture that fully recognizes the absurdity of the inverted world in which she finds herself. In her willful absurdity she has assumed a kind of heroic stance—one which was not granted to Danton and his friends. Yet we must also remember that Büchner depicts her as mad in her final scenes: only in madness, he implies, can one perform an act that has a meaning in a meaningless world.

3 *LEONCE AND LENA:* COMEDY AS A DIVERSION FROM DESPAIR

OF BÜCHNER'S FOUR WORKS, *Leonce and Lena* is the only one that takes its form from a recognizable generic tradition. It is a romantic comedy, and its roots are distantly in Shakespearean comedy, in the *commedia dell'arte,* in several comedies of the German Romantic Movement, and, most specifically, in the plays of Alfred de Musset. On the surface it looks like a fairly conventional romantic tale. A melancholy young prince is about to be forced to marry a princess whom he has never met. With the help of his servant Valerio he escapes the country and in a tavern accidentally meets the princess who, with the help of her governess, has also attempted to escape her fate. Neither knows who the other is, and they fall in love. Valerio brings them back to the prince's land and presents them, dressed as pasteboard effigies of themselves, to the court. The king marries them in effigy, their masks are removed, and prince and princess for the first time discover each other's true identity. At the end they seem about to live happily ever after. Or only seem to—for Büchner uses the conventions of romantic comedy only to confound them.

When one sets the play next to *As You Like It,* from which Büchner has drawn his epigraph for the first act, one is aware that in the course of imitating these conventions, Büchner has worked to undermine them. Prince Leonce, for example, turns out to be no more like a Shakespearean lover than Danton is like an Aristotelian tragic hero. He is less an Orlando than a Jaques who manages to amuse himself by assuming the manner of a Touchstone. The epigraph which Büchner chose—"O that I were a fool! / I am ambitious for a motley coat"—is, in fact, drawn from one of Jaques' speeches, in which the latter speaks of his meeting with Touchstone. Like the characters in Shakespeare's play Leonce escapes from an unsatisfactory everyday world into an ideal world, but the ideal world he chooses is nothing so substantial as the Forest of Arden; it is, rather, a private, inward world in which he seeks to distract himself with such activities as spitting on a stone 365 times in a row or trying to see the top of his head. The main representative of the real world in Büchner is not the tyrannical father of the *commedia dell'arte* tradition, but a bumbling, absurd king so lost in his own private world (a parody on Fichtean idealism) that he can hardly even remember the demand he makes on his son to get married. He consents to the marriage "in effigy" at the end only because he can justify it by his own absurd logic—"If you have a man hanged in effigy isn't that just as good as if he received a regulation hanging? . . . Now I have it. We'll celebrate the wedding in effigy."

The romance that takes place between the Prince of Popo and the Princess of Pipi (the names of the two kingdoms are affectionate slang terms, respectively, for *buttocks* and *urine*) is not precisely the romantic love out of which most comedies are made. The hero and heroine are never infatuated with one another in the usual way of comedies, nor is their relationship even based on their "being in love with love." If anything, their love seems to originate in a mutual feeling of compassion for each other's suffering. "I believe there are men who are unhappy, incurably so, merely because they exist," Lena says of Leonce, while the latter thinks himself moved by Lena's wistful plaint, "Is the way so long?" as she wearily enters the tavern. Leonce's declaration of love has none of the romantic enthusiasm one might expect, but is expressed in the most macabre imagery imaginable: "Then let me be your angel of death, let my lips swoop down upon your eyes like wings. [*He kisses her.*] Oh lovely dead body, you rest so charmingly on the black pall of night that Nature hates life and falls in love with death." After he has declared himself, instead of voicing his conviction that his love for her will last forever, he despairs of its ability to sustain itself and consequently decides to throw himself in a river. (Büchner does not, however, break the comic convention to the point of letting him go through with it, for Valerio immediately appears and talks him out of it.)

In Shakespearean romantic comedy and in the *commedia dell'arte* the youthful lovers are united in marriage at the end; the ideal world which they represent replaces a decadent or cruel "real" world; and we rest assured that they will live happily ever after. Büchner maneuvers his play at least formally through these steps, so shrewdly, in fact, that one of his finest critics was fooled into viewing the resolution as one of "serenity and joy, recognition and fulfillment." [1] Certainly King Peter, about to retire permanently into his dogmatic slumbers with his philosophical advisers, hands the reins of government to the newly wedded couple. But the brave new world which they intend to set up is scarcely to be taken at face value: "Well, Lena, have you noticed yet that our pockets are full of toys and dolls? What shall we do with them? Shall we make moustaches for the dolls and hang sabres on them? Or shall we dress them in tail coats and have them conduct miniature politics and diplomacy with us looking on through a microscope?"

Leonce, indeed, plans the same sort of absurd activities which he had engaged in—and quickly tired of—throughout the course of the play. And if Büchner needed to give us any further clues as to how seriously we should take Leonce's plans for a lotus land, he lets the ironic Valerio speak the last word:

> And I'll be Minister of State. And a decree will be issued that whoever gets calluses on his hands shall be placed under surveillance . . . whoever boasts that in the sweat of his brow he will eat bread shall be declared insane and dangerous to human society. And then we can lie in the

shade and ask God for macaroni, melons, and figs, for musical throats, classic bodies, and a nice, cosy religion!

The irony that lurks behind the language in which both Leonce and Valerio sketch out their idyllic future is obvious even without the last line if one has noted the similarly ironic perspective in which Büchner has clothed their longings throughout the play. But Valerio's final words about a "nice, cosy religion" break down any illusions we may have about a "happily ever after." In the light of such irony one is tempted to view in a double perspective the words which the prince and princess speak after their marriage, when each discovers who the other really is:

LENA I've been deceived.
LEONCE *I've* been deceived.
LENA O chance!
LEONCE O Providence!

On the surface these words can all be taken as signs of a happy resolution; in this sense the couple was happily deceived, and chance and Providence were gracious to them. But if one remains aware of the normally negative meaning of *deceived*, chance and Providence may not have been so kind to them after all. The play, at any rate, leaves both possibilities open; the first supports the romantic conventions Büchner is using, the second his ironic questioning of these conventions.

Not that irony was missing from Shakespearean comedy. But the irony of a Touchstone or a Feste, by putting the romanticism of the various lovers to a test throughout the play, serves in the end to confirm the positive assertions toward which the play has been moving (Touchstone, in fact, himself gets married at the end). Valerio's irony, on the other hand, merely continues to break down whatever illusions we may have that the ending is a happy one. But Valerio's function throughout the play cannot be described simply as that of the ironic fool. Leonce, after all, has assumed this role for himself at times. What is basic to the Leonce-Valerio relationship is the fact that they assume opposing roles toward one another. Whenever Leonce waxes romantic—for instance, in his attempt at a love-death suicide—Valerio cuts him ironically down to size. But whenever Leonce plays the ironist, Valerio sets up a series of romantic pretensions to break down Leonce's ironic pretensions, for example, in their first encounter in the play:

VALERIO I shall lie on the greensward and let my nose blossom above the blades of grass and get romantic notions when bees and butterflies light on it. . . .

LEONCE Don't breathe so hard, my dear fellow, or the bees and butterflies will starve: the flowers are their snuffbox, and you're taking great pinches of the snuff.

VALERIO Oh sir, how much feeling I have for Nature! . . .

The whole rhythm of the play, down to the final words, is based on Büchner's setting up illusions and then systematically breaking them down. Though he goes through all the motions of writing a romantic comedy—a genre which demands that romantic ideals eventually can become reality—he has, at bottom, written an ironic comedy—one in which ideals are shown up for the illusions they really are. It is as if Shakespeare had used the plot and atmosphere of *As You Like It* to create the mood and content of *Volpone*.

Although Büchner has rigorously kept up the forms of romantic comedy, the spirit of disillusionment which fills the play is more closely related to that of Büchner's most immediate model, Musset's *Fantasio*, than it is to anything in Shakespeare. Like *Leonce and Lena*, Musset's play has a sad princess about to be forced into marriage with a distant prince. The model for Leonce is not, however, the prince, but a village melancholic, Fantasio, who complains of his ennui, plans and rejects a multitude of activities, and finds a temporarily satisfying *métier* by disguising himself as a court jester. He is more languid, though also less desperate than Leonce, more sentimental and less incisively analytical about his plight than his German counterpart.[2]

Musset, too, borrows the conventions of romantic comedy, but, quite in contrast to Büchner, he refuses to resolve the play with the conventions he has used to shape it most of the way through. Thus, after employing a number of charming artifices—master and servant disguising as one another, the hero knocking off the villain's wig—Musset is unwilling to give us a happy ending. At the end the melancholy hero, recognizing he can never be happy in any occupation, refuses the princess' offer of a permanent appointment as jester. He goes his independent way, and the heroine, though he has saved her from a marriage she dreaded, is left to brood alone. As though he suddenly recognized the insincerity of his conventions, Musset—not only in *Fantasio,* but in the other two plays from which Büchner borrowed, *Marianne's Whims* and *One Shouldn't Trifle with Love*—at the last minute turns sincere and faces up to the problems of his characters as though he were writing a realistic play. The effect of this change is jarring, as if, after sitting through most of *As You Like It* or a Marivaux comedy, we ended up with the last act of *A Doll's House.* The surprise we experience at the end does not result from any new insights which the author uncovers for us—as, for instance, the surprises at the end of a Ionesco play do—but is the surprise we feel at suddenly being let down; we feel cheated, and wish that Musset had surprised us instead with more and better artifices. *Fantasio,* of course, lives by the charm of its language and atmosphere (charm is the word one inevitably uses when speaking of Musset's plays), not by its dramaturgy. And it is precisely in its dramaturgy that we see the superiority of *Leonce and Lena.* For Büchner recognized that a comedy is essentially a game, and that if he wished to adjust his comedy to his more serious purposes, he must at least pretend to abide by the rules of the game; the ironic undercurrent which runs through the play makes his serious purposes amply clear, but it does not prevent the game from moving to its logical conclusion.

ii

Being a game, the comic form that Büchner employed provided him with an appropriate image for the activities that his characters engage in: these characters do not live ordinary lives, but instead keep themselves busy playing games with life. And since a theater piece necessarily must express itself in words, Büchner found an appropriate image for these games in the punning and idle bantering in which his characters are constantly engaged. "O foul conception when you were conceived!" Leonce shouts at Valerio at one point. "Find yourself a better mode of expression or I'll give you an impression of all the oppression that I . . ."—the translation, though it cannot be entirely literal, succeeds at least in imitating the sort of word-play that goes on throughout the comedy. Leonce is by no means angry at Valerio when he addresses him in this way; the word-game he plays here and elsewhere becomes a sort of substitute for any real emotions he might feel. Quite often he—and Valerio as well—gets so lost in his verbal associations that these seem to have little if any reference to any real situation. He finds himself lost not only in words, but in images which he concocts in his mind. At one point he announces: "I have the image and ideal of a female in my head. I must go in quest of it. She is endlessly beautiful and endlessly mindless. Her beauty is as helpless and touching as a newborn infant's. Is the contrast not delightful—eyes both heavenly and dumb, a mouth both divine and moronic . . . ?"

There is no reason we need take Leonce's search for the ideal at all seriously; he is merely fascinated by the paradox suggested by his image, and he goes on to exploit this paradox until he gets bored with it. Even in his love scene with Lena language replaces relationship, for the contact between the two is realized on a linguistic level only. "Träume sind selig" (Dreams are blessed), says Lena, to which Leonce replies, "So träume Dich selig und lass mich Dein seliger Traum sein" (Then dream yourself blessed, and let me be your blessed dream). Leonce's words, in the German at least, are an exact repetition of Lena's words dreams and *blessed*, yet by changing the syntactical functions of these words (*Träume* is both a plural noun and an imperative verb, *selig* an adjective and an adverb), he gives the impression of a kind of miraculous transformation taking place. As one of Büchner's best commentators, Gerhart

Baumann, speaking of the play as a whole, has put it, "In its most dream-like moments it is the magic of the language that is working, while the characters become simply media." [3] At various points in the play the characters even resort to metaphors drawn from the vocabulary of linguistics. "When you bow, dear sir, your legs form a beautiful parenthesis," Leonce tells the court tutor, and in one of his verbal battles with Valerio, master accuses servant of being "begotten by the five vowels," while the latter retorts, "And you, my prince, are a book with no words in it, nothing but dashes."

If language can thus become a substitute for reality, the real world, in turn, at least as it is shown in the play, has little substantiality of its own. It is represented, after all, by the ridiculous king, while the local folk whom we are shown—for example, the schoolmaster—display an absurdity totally ungraced by wit. Valerio's description of one of the lands he and Leonce pass through provides a suitable enough comment on the real world that Leonce seeks to escape: "This country is like an onion—nothing but skins. Or Chinese boxes—one inside the other—in the biggest, nothing but boxes, in the smallest, nothing at all."

Behind all the banter it gradually becomes clear to us that the characters in the play are none too sure of their own identities. I mentioned earlier that Leonce and Valerio are constantly exchanging roles: when one of them plays the enthusiast, the other plays the ironist, and vice versa. Being uncertain who they are, they content themselves with the roles they assume; role-playing, moreover, helps kill time and diverts them from their real selves, whatever these may be. The traditional comic artifices which Büchner employs serve as ways of defining this theme. Thus, the fact that the lovers do not know each other's names is not only a convenient plot device, but it also suggests that such knowledge tells us very little about ourselves.

The knowledge that one must remain uncertain of his identity becomes a rather painful discovery in the context built up by the play. King Peter suggests the problem quite early in the text: "When I speak my thoughts aloud this way, I don't know who's speaking, myself or someone else. And this frightens me. [*After prolonged musing.*] I am I." But the king's attempt at self-assertion is obviously no solution to the problem. Valerio, when he removes a series of masks from his face, gives us a far more incisive answer. "Who are you?" the king asks him, and he replies "Do I know?" [*He slowly removes several masks, one after the other.*] Is this me? Or this? Or this? Shell the nut! Turn back the leaves! Really, I'm rather afraid I may peel myself completely away." The image in which he sees himself is essentially the onion or the Chinese boxes he had earlier used to describe the country he was passing through: behind the façade there is nothing at all. Leonce and Valerio find at least temporary diversions from this frightening discovery through the language games they play. But Lena, who is not so verbally endowed, must seek other means of escape; her solution is to identify herself with the vegetable world: "I should have been brought up in a pot like a plant, you know that. I need dew and night air, like flowers."

Büchner's most powerful suggestion about the true identities of his characters comes in the climactic scene, when Valerio leads in the lovers, disguised in pasteboard, whom he introduces as "The Two World-Famous Automata." In one sense the disguise is merely a part of the comic game, since after all it makes possible the marriage needed for a happy ending. But Valerio's speech describing the "automata" goes well beyond the exigencies of plot. Though wryly spoken, it presents an image of man reduced to something less than an animal, for he is totally devoid of will, yet fools himself into thinking he has chosen to cultivate moral ideals and civilized pleasures:

> Ladies and gentlemen, you see before you two persons of both the sexes, one little man and one little woman, a gentleman and a lady! It's all mechanism and art, all clock springs and pasteboard! Each of these two persons has a superfine ruby spring in his or her right foot just under the nail of his or her little toe, as the case may be. Give it a bit of a push, and the whole mechanism runs a full fifty years. . . . Take note of this, everyone, they have

> just come to a very interesting stage, at which stage a new mechanism manifests itself, the mechanism of love. The gentleman has carried the lady's shawl several times. The lady has averted her gaze several times and looked toward heaven. Both have more than once whispered: faith—love—hope. Both look very much as if an understanding had been arrived at. All that's lacking is the one very small word, Amen.

Through this, the longest single speech in the play, Leonce's earlier statements about the uselessness of all endeavor seem resoundingly confirmed, while his plans to lead an idyllic existence with Lena on an exotic Italian isle are set in an ironic perspective even before he can announce them.

For all its surface gaiety the play is centrally concerned with the exposure and analysis of Leonce's particular species of romantic agony. The most obvious manifestation of his disease is his boredom. "What people won't do out of boredom!" he soliloquizes in the opening scene. But his boredom is but one of many closely connected symptoms. Among other things he suffers from an intense self-consciousness which does not allow him to maintain any point of view without subjecting it to intense analysis and ultimately rejecting it. Though he identifies himself with Hamlet at one point (Act II, Scene 2), he is but one side of the real Hamlet: he is the introspective Hamlet which the nineteenth century often saw to the exclusion of other sides of Shakespeare's hero, an idle Hamlet, one might say, with absolutely no task to carry out. Valerio jokingly suggests a number of occupations to him—scientist, military hero, genius, being a "useful member of society"—but since he can see through them, he rejects them categorically; and he finds equal reason to reject the various preoccupations he flirts with in the course of the play—joker, drinker, romantic lover, or specialist in such pursuits as dissecting ants and counting the filaments of flowers. The only aim which he does not overtly reject is his dream of escape to a blissful southern never-never land, but within the context of the play we cannot believe he takes even this dream seriously.

He constantly maneuvers his thoughts into a vicious

circle: he recognizes the emptiness of his existence ("my life yawns at me like a great white piece of a paper that I should cover all over with writing, and I don't get a word written"); he admits the reality of his sufferings; but he also goes to great lengths to convince himself that every possible solution to his dilemma will not work for him. He is so self-conscious about his emotions that when he comes to generalize about his dilemma he must introduce his remarks with the line, "Come on, Leonce, do me a monologue, I'll be a good listener," and conclude them with a still more histrionic gesture: "Bravo, Leonce, bravo! [*He claps.*] It really does me good to call out to myself like this." He is, in fact, two (or more) selves—enthusiast one moment, ironist the next, seeking an end to his dilemma, and yet not seeking it; and, as Valerio's image of the masks suggests, one is none too sure what ultimate self stands behind all the others.

Among the selves which Leonce tries out on occasion is the sadist. "Gentlemen, gentlemen, do *you* know what Caligula and Nero were like? *I* do," he desperately exclaims in his most histrionic monologue. As with the Roman emperors whom he invokes, the transition from feeling bored to being cruel comes to seem a wholly natural one to him. He puts on this self in an early scene, well before his meeting with Lena: he is about to play the lover with a girl named Rosetta, for whom he sets up a romantic atmosphere with candlelight, music and wine; but when the girl enters, his only response to her is a yawn. Büchner, of course, never allows the comic artifice to break down by letting us pity the girl. But at the same time he refuses to gloss over Leonce's cruelty. He resolves the dramatic problem by letting Rosetta leave the scene singing, her disappointment stylized by the sadness of the words she sings.

The emotional state which Leonce proclaims most frequently is a feeling of indifference, an absence of real emotion. "To tired feet, every way is *too* long," he tells Lena, who soon after speaks of "spring on his cheeks, and winter in his heart." Words suggesting fatigue are used of and by him at innumerable points. Leonce, in short, is caught in a kind of living death. "The ticking of the death-watch beetle within our breasts is slow, every drop of our blood measures out its time, our life is a creeping fever"—these words of Leonce's might easily have come from *Danton's Death*. Amid the gaiety which Büchner keeps whipping up one almost fails to notice how often death is referred to; talk of death, in fact, is almost as dense in *Leonce and Lena* as in Büchner's earlier play. Valerio's description of the automata at the end of the play simply creates a memorable metaphor for the state of living death in which we have seen Leonce throughout. Büchner himself suggests a connection between the automaton image and the weary state of indifference he described in Leonce. In a letter written to his fiancée more than two years before—the same letter, indeed, in which he describes the powerful effect he felt from his study of the French Revolution—he speaks of the emptiness that overcame him after illness: "And now? And at other times? I do not feel even the ecstasy of pain and yearning. Since crossing the bridge over the Rhine, I am as though annihilated within myself, not a single emotion rises in me. I am an automaton; my soul has been taken from me."[4]

Death

The sickness he portrays so vividly in Leonce was by no means a new phenomenon in literature at the time he wrote the play. Its literary roots go back at least to Rousseau and its basic symptoms fill the works of many German Romantics of a generation before, not to speak of contemporary French and English models, above all Musset. What separates Büchner from his predecessors is the thoroughness with which he has analyzed the disease and his refusal to sentimentalize it in any way. A passage such as the following, in which Musset's Fantasio (who otherwise has many symptoms in common with Leonce) romanticizes the simple life he had seen pictured in a Flemish painting, would be inconceivable in Büchner:

> A young woman on the threshold, the lighted fire which one sees at the back of the room, supper prepared, the children asleep; all the tranquility of the peaceful and contemplative life in a corner of the picture! And the man

> still short of breath but steady in the saddle. . . . The good woman follows him with her eyes for a minute and then, returning to her fire, utters that sublime blessing of the poor: "May God protect him!" [Act 1, Scene 2]

Leonce's corresponding dream is the southern idyll he plans with Lena at the end:

> We'll have all the clocks smashed and all the calendars suppressed, then we'll count the hours and the moons only by the flowers, by blossom and fruit. And then we'll surround our little country with burning lenses, so there'll be no more winter, and in summer the heat will shoot us clear up to Ischia and Capri by a process of distillation. And so we'll spend the whole year among roses and violets, oranges and laurel.

Leonce describes his longings with such outrageous extravagance that we view them critically even without the ironic perspective which Valerio introduces directly after. The rigor with which Büchner maintains the comic conventions works as a guarantee that the sentiments his characters express will maintain their proper distance from author and audience.

Through this very distance Büchner's approach to the sickness he describes has far less in common with that of his predecessors than with that of a writer such as Kierkegaard. Kierkegaard, who was Büchner's exact contemporary and no mean comic artist himself, did not begin writing until well after Büchner's death and was of course unaware of the German writer's work. Yet the affinities between the two writers, as Gustav Beckers has demonstrated with painstaking detail in his book-length study of *Leonce and Lena*, are considerable.[5] For instance, Leonce, in his ambivalent attitude toward himself, his fascination for atmospheric effect, his constant search for distraction from boredom, his role-playing, his cruelty, his unwillingness to be burdened with any sort of commitment, is a model example of the phenomenon which Kierkegaard diagnosed as the "aesthetic" stage of life. Büchner, of course, does not postulate an "ethical" or a "religious" point of view through which to look at the aesthetic one; he does not, like Kierkegaard, create a larger dialectical system, but simply presents Leonce's dilemma with the characteristic tools of a comic dramatist. Indeed, it is through his success as a dramatist—in his unrelentingly ironic perspective, his manipulation of traditional comic devices—that this dilemma speaks to us with a contemporary relevance that we do not find in most other nineteenth-century accounts of the same phenomenon.

Leonce's view of life, one scarcely need add, in many respects re-echoes Danton's (as it, in turn, parallels that of such other Büchner characters as Lenz and the captain in *Woyzeck*). Yet Büchner creates far different dramatic contexts for Danton and Leonce, with the result that our attitudes toward their respective dilemmas are quite different. Danton's disillusionment is confirmed, as it were, by the inverted world of the Reign of Terror which surrounds and engulfs him; the irony with which he interprets this world is to a great degree, though not wholly, the point of view of the play. Leonce's irony, on the other hand, is constantly placed within other ironical perspectives, both by himself and by other characters; he serves at once as spokesman for the play and as comic butt. Above all, Büchner does not, in *Leonce and Lena*, struggle with the larger questions which give *Danton's Death* so vast a scope. He often enough suggests such questions in his comedy, for instance when Valerio, interrupting the court chaplain in the marriage ceremony, announces, "It was before the creation of the world . . . God was bored—." But these questions are kept carefully within comic bounds; the desperateness with which they are asked in the Conciergerie scenes of *Danton's Death* remains well outside the scope of the comedy. Although *Leonce and Lena*, then, does not strive to move us with the overwhelming force of the earlier play, the comic forms within which it works still provide a most appropriate vehicle for the attitudes which emerge from the text: by using comic routines which imply that nothing need be taken seriously Büchner found a way of expressing the painful discovery that nothing *can* be taken seriously.

4 LENZ: INTERNAL DRAMA AND THE FORM OF FICTION

BÜCHNER'S STORY *Lenz* is as bold an innovation in narrative prose as *Danton's Death* and *Woyzeck* are in drama. Its uniqueness does not lie either in its basic theme or in the genre—the *Novelle*—which Büchner chose for his material. Its subject—a man struggling with insanity—was scarcely new in German fiction by Büchner's time. During the Romantic period German writers had often dealt with aberrational states—for instance, Achim von Arnim in *The Mad Invalide* (1818), whose title character, possessed by irrational forces, terrorizes a town by shooting from a nearby fort, and E. T. A. Hoffmann in *Knight Gluck* (1808), whose hero fancies himself the composer Gluck. The characteristic triumphs of German prose writers could, indeed, be described by their essentially introspective concerns and their experimentation in shorter forms. The German-speaking countries, in contrast to England and France, have had no long-standing tradition of serious novels which define their heroes primarily through their relationship to their social milieu, as do the novels of Jane Austen or Stendhal; the most notable tradition in longer German fiction is, in fact, the so-called *Bildungsroman*, a form which, from Goethe's *Wilhelm Meister* to Thomas Mann's *Magic Mountain*, has taken for its theme the emotional and intellectual development of the young man of sensibility. Up to the time of Kafka and Mann Germany produced exceptionally few novels of the first order; the finest examples of German narrative prose are largely in the *Novelle* form, which varies in length from the short story to what we would consider a short novel. The many masterpieces in this form which appeared during the generation before Büchner were written in the most sharply divergent styles—for example, the genial and courtly manner of Goethe's story entitled simply *Novelle* (1827) the grotesqueness and fantasy of Hoffmann's tales, the breathlessly tense and strained narration of Heinrich von Kleist's stories.

Although much German fiction before Büchner—notably Goethe's *Novelle* and the wildly organized novels of Jean Paul—shows great technical daring, Büchner's story represents a distinct break with all that came before him, both in the techniques it employs and in the effects it achieves through these techniques. For *Lenz* anticipates many of the techniques which one associates primarily with modern fiction, most conspicuously, perhaps, in its essential plotlessness. What "plot" there is consists of the psychological ups and downs that take place during a few weeks in the life of the hero, the poet and dramatist Lenz, who, suffering from periodic attacks of insanity, at the time of the story is shown in the care of a celebrated Alsatian pastor, Johann Friedrich Oberlin (1740–1826). A nineteenth-century reader might well have taken it for a case-history rather than a literary work. And in a sense it *is* a case-history, for Büchner drew his material largely from the observations which Oberlin had scrupulously recorded in his diary and which Büchner's Strasbourg friends, the Stöber brothers, had made available to him.

The real-life Lenz (1751–92) was one of the great *poètes maudits* of German literature. He had a brief period of fame during the Storm-and-Stress period of the 1770's, but his work soon fell into obscurity. A collected edition of his writings which appeared in 1828, during Büchner's school years, temporarily revived interest in him. Goethe treated him rather harshly in his autobiography, describing him as one who had "surpassed all the idle and half idle young men who were destroying themselves inwardly and suffered from that phenomenon of the time depicted in the figure of Werther" (*Poetry and Truth*, Book XIV). Goethe, who goes on to describe him as an expert in intrigue, had good reason, perhaps, to present the world with an unfavorable portrait. From the time Lenz had met Goethe during the latter's students days in Strasbourg, he had been desperately envious both of Goethe's genius as a writer and his relative stability of character. He was, in fact, commonly ridiculed as "Goethe's ape." He not only imitated his works, but, after Goethe had left Strasbourg, attempted, unsuccessfully, to court Friederike Brion, with whom Goethe had earlier had a romantic attachment. (In Büchner's story the hero, still obsessed with the memory of Friederike, in his madness confuses her with a dying young girl and tries to awaken the corpse of a baby who bore the same first name). During the succeeding years Lenz received Goethe's help in finding publishers for his writings and developed a childlike infatuation for Goethe's sister, who with her husband looked after him for a time in their home. After Goethe had settled in the court of Weimar in 1775 Lenz even followed him there, with the unhappy result that, because of Lenz' social ineptness, Goethe secured lodgings for him well outside the town. As his insanity was setting in he was cared for in Switzerland by a philanthropic doctor, Christoph Kaufmann (who appears briefly in Büchner's story), whom he had met through Goethe and who, in turn, sent him to Oberlin's home, in an isolated small community, the Steintal, near Strasbourg. The story opens with Lenz' arrival in the community late in January, 1778, and ends with his departure, under close surveillance, early the next month for Strasbourg, after Oberlin, as a result of Lenz' declining condition, felt compelled to let him go. After the events of the story his condition temporarily improved, but during his remaining years, largely spent in his native Lithuania, he suffered frequent breakdowns; he was found dead, under obscure circumstances, on a street in Moscow.

I have filled in all this background precisely because Büchner was compelled to leave it out through the demands of the technique he was using. The story is told from Lenz' point of view; although it is in the third person, we view the events almost wholly (but not quite) as Lenz sees them, without direct comment from the author. Thus, the characters are not identified or introduced in any way except as they appear through the eyes of the hero or in the few passages of conversation recorded in the story. Right from the start, in fact, Büchner establishes a tone of matter-of-fact concreteness:

> On the 20th of January Lenz went across the mountains. The summits and the high slopes covered with snow, gray stones all the way down to the valleys, green plains, rocks and pine-trees.
>
> It was damp and cold; water trickled down the rocks and gushed over the path. The branches of the pine-trees drooped heavily in the moist air. . . . Indifferently he moved on; the way did not matter to him, up or down. He felt no tiredness, only sometimes it struck him as unpleasant that he could not walk on his head.

The whole scene is presented to us as Lenz experiences it. Connectives are largely missing ("gray stones all the way down to the valleys, green plains, rocks and pine-trees"), for Büchner is attempting to dramatize the process of perception, which for Lenz consists of observation to the exclusion of logical reflection. Similarly to such modern writers as Hemingway and Camus, Büchner recognizes that the reader puts more faith in objects and sensations themselves than in the author's interpretation of them. Thus, by the time we reach the end of the above passage we have so fully participated in Lenz' point of view that we accept without question his disgruntlement at his not being able to walk on his head. Lenz' odd desire is presented just as matter-of-factly as his observation of the landscape around him: in the context Büchner has established the aberrational comes to seem entirely natural. Indeed, if *Lenz* is in one respect a case-study, it is no more so than many modern works—Camus' *Stranger* or Kafka's *Trial*, for instance—which refuse to comment directly on their heroes, but merely appear to present the relevant data through these heroes' eyes.

Büchner apparently discovered what was not generally discovered in European literature until well after his time—that inward emotional states can be rendered most convincingly in a sober, objective manner and, moreover, that the simplest, least intentionally "literary" way of narrating an event can sometimes be the most artistically powerful one.

The objective manner of presentation which Büchner follows so scrupulously in *Lenz* was no doubt suggested by his source. Oberlin's diary jottings, though sympathetic toward Lenz in their general tone, are a detailed, but also concise record of their subject's activities in the Steintal; the observations, one might say, are largely allowed to speak for themselves.[1] Büchner relied on his source not only for its objective manner and the events it recorded, but—as he had done with Robespierre's speeches in *Danton's Death*—he lifted whole sections literally from his source. Roughly an eighth of the story's less than 10,000 words, in fact, are Oberlin's. The following lines, except for the omission of one inconsequential word, are copied directly from the diary: "He visited the grave of the child whom he had once tried to raise from the dead, knelt down several times, kissed the earth on the grave, seemed to be praying, but confusedly plucked up some of the flowers that grew on the grave, to keep as a souvenir, returned to Waldbach, turned back again, and Sebastian with him."

Through the factual dryness with which Lenz' actions were recorded Büchner is able to maintain a sense of dignity for his hero while at the same time placing his irrational behavior in full view. (The common pitfall for a writer dealing with insanity is to render the hero either absurd or pitiful.) The reportorial tightness of this passage, achieved as it is through the succession of parallel phrases ("knelt down several times, kissed the earth on the grave, seemed to be praying"), anticipates an effect which Flaubert was later to make one of the most recognizable characteristics of his similarly concise, seemingly objective style; and as with Flaubert, the tightness and objectivity are signs of Büchner's refusal to indulge in unwarranted emotions or empty rhetoric. The antirhetorical view which Danton upheld against the verbal irresponsibilities of Robespierre and St. Just in *Lenz* becomes the view which the author imposes over all his material. Büchner drew not only such dryly factual passages as the above quotation from Oberlin's account, but he also borrowed some of Lenz' own words from his source. Most of the conversations in the story—with the obvious exception of Lenz' lengthy discussion of aesthetics, which Büchner composed—are also from the diary, including the hero's most impassioned and irrational outburst, in which he expresses his emotions on the death of the girl he confuses with Friederike Brion: "Oh, she's dead! Is she still alive? You angel! She loved me, I loved her, she was worthy of it—you angel! This damnable jealousy, I sacrificed her—she loved another man also—I loved her, she was worthy of it—O dear mother, she also loved me. I'm a murderer!"

The matter-of-fact context which surrounds this passage in both the diary and the story serves to set Lenz' ravings at an appropriate distance from the reader. Yet these ravings (given what we are told of Lenz' condition) also retain a certain conversational naturalness, and the credit for this surely belongs to Oberlin, who refused to embellish his subject's words with the rhetorical flourishes in which most men of his time would have been tempted to indulge.

The reportorial flatness and naturalness which Büchner found in his source were not enough in themselves to create a work of art. They remain, rather, a kind of grounding which Büchner needed as a base for psychological explorations which were well beyond the grasp of Oberlin, at least as his personality emerges from the diary. The Oberlin we see in the diary and in the story is immensely well-meaning, but unimaginative and somewhat obtuse: confronted with Lenz' ravings he can return nothing but stock clerical responses (the real-life Oberlin, who was one of the most progressive pastors of his time and who is still immortalized in the name of a well-known American college, may well have been superior to the portrait he gave of himself in his diary). It was necessary for Büchner, first of all, to shift from Oberlin's to Lenz' point of view; yet he did not go so far as to let Lenz narrate the events in the first person. By retaining a third-person method, he could alternately dip into Lenz' innermost thoughts and describe Lenz' actions with the tone of sobriety he had found in his source—a tone, moreover, which he needed to set Lenz' raging emotions in a proper perspective. One can discern the extremes between which he alternated in the following lines: "He spoke, he sang, he recited passages from Shakespeare, he clutched at everything that at another time would have made his blood flow more quickly, he tried everything, but cold, cold! He had to go out into the open air."

The opening words, with their short parallel phrases, maintain the cool stance of Oberlin's diary. But in the course of the succeeding lines we feel the author probing gradually more deeply into Lenz' frantic mind; by the time he reaches the phrase "He tried everything," though it is in the third person, he has made the language imitate something of Lenz' desperation. With the words "Cold, cold," he has temporarily abandoned any pretense of third-person technique. Yet almost as soon as he has let Lenz speak out directly he returns to the detached tone of the beginning. In passages such as this, as Walter Höllerer has pointed out, Büchner reveals himself as one of the pioneers in the discovery of interior monologue in fiction.[2] By moving alternately into and out of his character's mind, Büchner had the double advantage of presenting Lenz' mental processes in all their immediacy while at the same time refusing to let his hero take over the narrative responsibility himself. Büchner's method here is perhaps the narrative equivalent of the "objective" dramatic method I noted in his plays, in which the views of heroes like Danton and Leonce are qualified by those of the other characters and by the whole surrounding context.

The illusion of objectivity which Büchner achieves both in his plays and in *Lenz* is much the same illusion which many writers, from Flaubert onwards, have sought to achieve in narrative prose. Modern criticism in fact has sometimes employed the word "dramatic" to describe the novelist's achievement of this illusion. When Joyce, for instance, in his *Portrait of the Artist* distinguishes between the lyric, epic and dramatic genres, he does not base his definitions on the "external" form of these genres, but rather on the relationship which the author expresses or implies toward his material. The dramatic artist, as Joyce defines him, is essentially the novelist of the Flaubertian tradition, the artist who, "like the God of the creation, remains within or behind or beyond or above his handiwork, invisible, refined out of existence, indifferent, paring his fingernails." [3] Joyce's memorable image of the artist-God paring his fingernails is, I think, an appropriate description of the stance which Büchner as author assumes; *Lenz,* though it is his only nontheatrical work, has something of the same "dramatic" quality as his plays.

But *Lenz* is dramatic in an even more fundamental sense. By dispensing with a fable and confining himself to the day-by-day actions and sensations of his hero, Büchner has made the story re-enact the drama raging within Lenz' mind. As Hermann Pongs, in one of the relatively few studies of the story, has put it, Lenz' mind becomes a kind of "theater in which the light and dark forces of human existence struggle with one another." [4] We sometimes speak of earlier fiction, such as Kleist's, as being dramatic, but the drama in a story like *Michael Kohlhaas* (1808) issues from conflicts between the characters and manifests itself through essentially external events; the tensions within the hero are defined for us principally through the role he plays in the fable which Kleist has placed him in. In *Lenz,* on the other hand, the drama is wholly internalized within the hero's mind. It is appropriate, indeed, that Büchner did not choose a theatrical framework for his material, for the internal events which he sought to explore could not have been presented with the same fullness or intricacy which his narrative method made possible; even Danton and Leonce, complex as they are for characters in a play, are not presented to us as intimately as Lenz. It seems natural, moreover, that Büchner should develop this narrative method to represent the essentially passive type of hero who most interested him, for the inward mental activity which the method uncovers creates an area for dramatic action which more than compensates for his external passivity.

By substituting psychological activity for the more external activity in which the Aristotelian hero customarily engaged, Büchner in Lenz anticipated a type of hero and a type of dramatic action which later novelists, like Dostoevski in his underground man, or Kafka in his nearly anonymous heroes, were to explore with far greater fullness and intensity. In a recent memorial notice on William Faulkner, Allen Tate described Faulkner as "one of the great exemplars of the international school of fiction which for more than a century has reversed the Aristotelian doctrine that tragedy is an action, not a quality. . . . Faulkner's great subject, as it was Flaubert's and Proust's, is passive suffering, the victim being destroyed either by society or by dark forces within himself." [5] Although we are accustomed to think of Büchner as a figure in the history of drama, by virtue of *Lenz* he holds a place in this narrative tradition described by Tate, a tradition which, well after his own time, was to become the mainstream of European fiction and, it could be argued, the mainstream of European letters as a whole.

ii

The forces at war within Lenz determine the organization of the story more than any of the external events which take place in it. The plot of the story, if there is a plot at all, is simply the sequence of Lenz' moods, which change from moment to moment with astounding rapidity. The moods out of which the story is built do not follow any random order, but move from one extreme to the other almost with the regularity of a pendulum. One could speak of a play of opposites which governs Büchner's narrative structure. The following passage, for instance, illustrates this movement from a moment of ecstasy through an intense depression and thence again toward a feeling of wellbeing:

. . . He thought that he must draw the storm into himself, contain it all within him, he stretched himself out and lay on the earth, dug his way into the All, it was an ecstasy that hurt him—or he rested and laid his head into the moss and half-closed his eyes, and then it withdrew, away, far away from him, the earth receded from him, became small as a wandering star and dipped down into a roaring stream which moved its clear waters beneath him. But these were only moments; then, soberly, he would rise, resolute, calm, as though a silhouetted drama had passed before his eyes—he remembered nothing.

Toward evening he came to the highest point of the mountain range, to the snow field from which one descended again into the flat country in the west; he sat down on the top. It had grown calmer toward evening; the cloud formations, constant and motionless, hung in the sky; as far as the eyes could reach, nothing but summits from which broad stretches of land descended, and everything so still, so gray, lost in twilight. He experienced a feeling of terrible loneliness; he was alone, quite alone. He wanted to talk to himself, but he could not, he hardly dared to breathe; the bending of his feet sounded like thunder beneath him, he had to sit down. He was seized with a nameless terror in this nothingness: he was in the void! He leaped to his feet and rushed down the slope.

It had grown dark, heaven and earth were melting into one. It seemed as though something were following him, as though something horrible must catch up with him, something that men cannot bear, as though madness on horseback were chasing him.

At last he heard voices; he was relieved, his heart grew lighter. He was told that another half-hour would see him to Waldbach.

He passed through the village. Lights shone in the windows, he looked inside as he went by: children at table, old women, girls, all with quiet, composed faces. It seemed to him that it was these faces that radiated light; he began to feel quite cheerful.

I have quoted at length because the movement of Lenz' moods from one extreme to the other is discernible only in larger segments such as this. This movement, moreover, is representative of the story as a whole. In this particular passage the opposing extremes of mood can be classified in diverse formulations—for Lenz hovers between feelings of activity ("he must draw the storm into himself") and passivity ("as though something were following him"); between calm ("his heart grew lighter") and fear ("he was seized with a nameless terror"); between a sense of communion ("he must contain it all within him") and separation ("he experienced a feeling of terrible loneliness").

In other parts of the story the dichotomies within which he moves can be described in still other ways: moments of religious faith and disbelief; feelings of inward fulfillment and emptiness; lightness and heaviness; solipsism and claustrophobia. Similar dichotomies prevail in the landscapes, which are alternately bleak and burgeoning with life, oppressive and benign. Since we see these landscapes only through Lenz' eyes, we are never quite sure if they influence Lenz' changes of mood, or if Lenz simply reads into the landscape what his mood demands. Both these alternatives are in a sense true: nature serves both as an index to and an influence on his moods. In the first paragraph of the above passage Lenz experiences a violent change of mood within a single, unchanging landscape; at other times, especially when sunlight or moonlight suddenly breaks in upon a stormy scene, the change in the landscape effects a change in his mood. Light, in fact, almost constantly acts as a positive force for Lenz; at the end of the above passage, for example, the lights in the windows and the light "radiating" from people's faces finally break his depression.

Despite the extremes which characterize Lenz' moods, one cannot simply label them "positive" or "negative." His joyful moods, for example, range widely in character from the childlike passivity he sometimes feels when Oberlin is calming him down, to the energetic interaction in which he engages with the landscape at the beginning of the above passage. In the same way his negative moods range from the passivity he feels when outside forces seem to be oppressing him, to a stance of aggressive, blaspheming anger. Moreover, Lenz is capable of interpreting the same phenomenon in opposite ways: at times he looks at Oberlin's pastoral life as a source of joy, at other times he condemns it as boring and meaningless.

If there is any progression in the story, it exists in the fact that Lenz' darker moods gradually come to predominate. In the final pages, for instance, the alternation of moods is less between "lighter" and "darker" than between the more active and passive extremes of Lenz' dark moods. In the final lines, as he is being carted to Strasbourg, his mood is one of blank, dull passivity; he is oblivious even to the moonlight, which up to this point has exerted a generally benign effect upon him:

> It grew darker as they approached Strasbourg; a high, full moon, all the more distant landmarks in darkness, only the mountain nearest to them still in sharp relief; the earth was like a golden cup over which the gold waves of the moon ran foaming. Lenz stared at it all, not an idea, not an emotion inside him; only a blunted fear that grew more intense as the landmarks lost themselves more and more in the darkness.

The image of the moon as it appears here is perhaps the most memorable nature image in the story. But it is memorable above all because it exists so fully independent of the unperceiving Lenz at this point. Yet Büchner refuses to resolve the story on this dark note. The last words he set down, "So he lived on . . ." hint that the succession of changing moods we have witnessed throughout the story will simply continue.[6] But no final resolution (in the old-fashioned sense) was possible, unless the story were to end with the hero's death. The very inconclusiveness with which it ends is part of the point that Büchner is making: the inward forces which afflict Lenz are an uncontrollable fate which the forces of the external world—symbolized by the good-hearted Oberlin and by Lenz' conscious mind as well—are powerless either to alleviate or comprehend. The resolution which follows most logically from the facts as they are presented is no resolution at all: "So he lived on . . ."

The benign forces which, temporarily at least, promise to

better Lenz' condition are symbolized by an image which had exerted a powerful influence in European literature at least since the time of Rousseau—the image of the "simple life," of peasants living well-ordered lives amid age-old communal traditions and led by a dedicated, kindly pastor. In the long passage from which I quoted above, Lenz' disposition improves as soon as he sees the "children at table, old women, girls, all with quiet, composed faces." The quietness is a sign of the stability for which he longs; a kind of quietude, in fact, comes over him as soon as he thinks he has made contact with these people. Thus, when Oberlin allows him to deliver a sermon to them, or when he accompanies Oberlin on his pastoral duties to a nearby village, his mood is described by words and phrases such as "beneficent," "immense repose," "harmonious," "a sweet sensation of infinite well-being."

Lenz desires not only to make contact with other human beings, but to create relationships which the reader quickly realizes as humanly impossible—for instance, his fascination with the fate of the dying girl whom he confuses with Friederike, or his obsession to revive the dead baby. These relationships are, in fact, an extension of his larger desire to interpenetrate and merge himself with the forces of nature as a whole. His drive to merge with nature was evident, for example, in his ecstatic experience described at the beginning of the long passage quoted earlier. His twin desires to interpenetrate with the human and the natural realms are brought together in the following discussion he holds with Oberlin:

> He went on: the simplest and purest individuals were most closely related to the elements; the more subtle a man's intellectual life and perceptions, the more blunted this sense of the elemental became. . . . He thought it must give one a sense of infinite bliss to be . . . touched by the individual life of every form of creation, to have a soul that would communicate with stones, metals, water and plants, as in a dream to absorb into oneself every being in nature.

The same desire to interpenetrate with simple, elemental beings becomes the basis for the views on aesthetics which he voices when he upholds realistic against idealized art in his discussion with Oberlin and Kaufmann: "One must love human nature in order to penetrate into the peculiar character of any individual." But Lenz' immense desire to love is obviously doomed from the start. His experiences in nature are at best temporary ones—indeed, the ecstasy he feels in nature changes all too quickly into fear. The simple human beings in whom he places such great hopes for his well-being ultimately have no real contact with him. In his discussion of aesthetics he describes in detail two Dutch or Flemish genre paintings, which, he claims, affect him far more deeply than the Apollo Belvedere or a Raphael Madonna. These genre paintings emerge from his discussion with much the same features as the real-life genre scenes he sees around him in Oberlin's village. Real life, at best, is something essentially pictorial for him. He observes the real-life scenes as lovingly as he observes the paintings, yet he can participate actively in neither. He remains the perpetual observer.

If Oberlin presides, as it were, over the benign world of simple beings, there is another character, a faith-healer, who, though he appears only in the scene in which Lenz visits the young girl, exercises a kind of demonic effect upon the protagonist. He is described through his "restless, troubled face," and his effect on the young girl is to make her "restless." The word which Büchner uses—*unruhig*—is, in fact, the opposite of the word which Büchner had often used earlier to characterize Oberlin and his world; for instance, in one passage describing Oberlin's effect on Lenz the German text employs the word *ruhig* (or its derivatives) three times in a single sentence. The whole atmosphere surrounding the healer (who was not even present in Büchner's source) stands in obvious contrast to the atmosphere of Oberlin's world. "His eyes met a lighted picture on the wall and remained fixed upon it, without a flicker" —thus Büchner describes the healer—"the people told Lenz that the man had come to this district a long time ago, no one knew where from, he was reputed to be a saint, he could see water underground and exorcise evil spirits, and people went on pilgrimages to see him."

From this point onwards, as Pongs has suggested in his

essay on the story, Lenz' darker moods begin to predominate.[7] But Büchner supplies no causal connections: at most he tells us, "He [Lenz] now felt uneasy in the presence of that powerful man, who sometimes seemed to him to be talking in horrible tones." The healer, one might say, was simply a catalyst for tendencies which we have seen within Lenz from the beginning. From here on, however, Lenz undergoes a succession of demonic moods—feverish dreams, claustrophobia, and, in one of the most memorable passages of the story, righteous anger at God:

> He felt capable of clenching an enormous fist, thrusting it up into heaven, seizing God and dragging Him through His clouds; capable of masticating the world with his teeth and spitting it into the face of the Creator; he swore, he blasphemed. Thus he arrived at the highest point of the mountains, and the uncertain light stretched down toward the white masses of stone, and the heavens were a stupid blue eye, and the moon, quite ludicrous, idiotic, stood in the midst. Lenz had to laugh loudly, and as he laughed atheism took root in him and possessed him utterly, steadily, calmly, relentlessly.

Even the landscape, at least as Lenz perceives it here, becomes eerie and demonic. Indeed, in such a passage we become aware of the very thin line which separates the case history from a record of visionary experience. Büchner's psychological realism, by a strange paradox, provided a means for the supernatural to remain in literature. Büchner's, indeed, is the only method with which the modern mind can accept and experience the furies which earlier poets such as Aeschylus were able to embody in directly visible form.

In his self-dividedness Lenz is in certain respects a late version of a type of hero who had been playing a predominant role in European literature for well over half a century. Through his violently opposed moods, he all too easily recalls a vast succession of inwardly torn heroes, from Werther and René to heroes of more lofty aspiration. At one point in *The Prelude* Wordsworth speaks of "Having two natures in me, joy the one / The other melancholy," while Faust's pronouncement about the "two souls" that dwell together in his breast is one of the more memorable tags in Goethe's drama. What separates Lenz emphatically from earlier Romantic heroes is that he is never romanticized. Some of his self-images, certainly, are part of the stock-in-trade of European Romanticism, for instance, his conception of himself as Satan or as the Wandering Jew. Yet when Lenz thinks of himself in such terms, the reader never feels himself bullied into assenting to these evaluations, as he is, for example, to those of Byron's various heroes, Oriental and otherwise. The context with which Büchner surrounds such pronouncements insures a detachment of author from character, and of character from reader. When Lenz declares to Oberlin, "I'm damned for eternity, I'm the Wandering Jew," Büchner follows this statement with the flat lines, "Oberlin told him that this was precisely what Jesus had died for, that he should turn to Him with fervor and would then partake of His mercy." By juxtaposing Lenz' impassioned outcry with the pastor's uncomprehending reply, Büchner sets both characters at an appropriately ironic distance from us. The irony which we find in this story does not issue from Lenz' own pronouncements (as it does from those of such other Büchner heroes as Danton and Leonce), but from the objective narrative method which Büchner pursues so rigorously. As a result of this method he is able to suggest that Lenz' various spiritual commitments—for instance his belief in the "simple life" or his occasional satanism—are not to be taken as views which the story itself propounds (as they are in most Romantic texts), but are simply projections of the hero's changing psychological condition.

Although Lenz himself does not share Danton's and Leonce's ironical propensities, at one point he speaks words almost identical to theirs. When Oberlin tells him to "direct his thoughts toward God," Lenz undercuts him with a discourse on the uselessness and boredom of such endeavors: "If I were as fortunate as you are, fortunate enough to find such a pleasant pastime, yes, in that case I imagine you could fill in the time quite pleasantly. All out of idleness:

for most of us pray out of boredom, others fall in love out of boredom."

Needless to say, Büchner did not draw these words (nor, for that matter, the landscape descriptions or any of Lenz' interior monologue) from his source. But these words strike us with a far different effect than do the corresponding passages in *Danton's Death* and *Leonce and Lena*; they are totally lacking in wryness or tact, but are spoken with cruelty and uncontrolled desperation. Although Büchner's narrative method allows him to exercise a certain degree of irony, *Lenz* is his only work without a trace of comedy. Its somberness is relieved only momentarily by Lenz' manic moods, which we recognize as deceptive from the start. By limiting the scope of the story and concentrating on Lenz' frenzied inward processes, Büchner was able to create at least the illusion of a mysterious world of images and sensations behind the world of normal perceptions. It is significant that Büchner, in a letter announcing his plans for the story, spoke of Lenz as "half mad" ("halb verrückt"): [8] he could thus place Lenz in two worlds at once, the everyday world of the reader (who would otherwise be unable to make contact with him), and the private world which Lenz shaped out of his own mind. The dark and teeming images that issue from this private world have a substance and a reality which, despite Büchner's refusal to commit himself to any transcendental beliefs, often seem to belie the naturalistic premises upon which his technique is built.

5 *WOYZECK:* TOWARDS DRAMA AS POETIC IMAGE

COMPARING Büchner's two tragic plays is like comparing two stages in the development of modern art. Next to *Woyzeck, Danton's Death,* for all its deviations from the German Classical drama, still has the appearance of a drama in the grand style, with long orations and great personages facing up to moments of the highest historical significance. Although Danton is unique in dramatic literature as a passive hero, he is also a figure whose past attainments are fully acknowledged in the play and who contemplates his death with an eloquent flow of words. The soldier Woyzeck is not only a passive hero, victimized as he is by his superiors, his mistress, and by society, but he is scarcely articulate and, in fact, at the edge of madness; compared to Woyzeck, the burgher-heroes of Ibsen's plays, for example, seem masters of eloquence and, at least within their own narrow worlds, unquestionably qualify for Aristotelian high station.

In *Woyzeck* the dramatic method which Büchner developed in *Danton's Death* is taken to what would appear its ultimate extreme. The earlier drama may well have seemed unique for the large number of short scenes out of which it is composed; *Woyzeck* contains almost as many scenes, yet is only one third as long a play. In both dramas the characters (with the exception of a few characters in *Woyzeck*) seem to have an objective existence of their own, quite independent of their creator's biases and whims; they reveal themselves through their peculiarities of language and their contrasts with one another. The characters of *Danton's Death*, even so spontaneous a being as Marion, reveal themselves in long, coherent speeches; the characters of *Woyzeck*, even in their monologues, tend to speak in phrases, often scarcely connected to one another. The contrasts between personalities, ways of speaking, and types of scenes through which *Danton's Death* discloses its meaning are expressed more tersely, more indirectly in *Woyzeck*; in the latter play Büchner comes to depend far more heavily than in *Danton's Death* on symbols, fragments of songs, or individual words which are taken up with varying meanings by different characters.

Woyzeck, in fact, is organized with much of the complexity and conciseness which we have come to associate with twentieth-century poetry. A paraphrase of its plot would reveal little of its essential tone or stature. To summarize it is to retell the story of a sordid, lower-class *crime passionnel:* a lowly soldier, Franz Woyzeck, supports his mistress and child doing odd jobs such as gathering firewood, shaving his captain, and playing guinea pig to a doctor who is experimenting with the effects of diet on urine; the mistress, Marie, is seduced by a drum major of Woyzeck's regiment; Woyzeck, after being ridiculed as a cuckold by the captain and doctor and beaten up in a fight by the drum major, stabs Marie to death and soon after drowns himself.

Only a few of the twenty-six or -seven scenes are centrally concerned with furthering the plot line as I have described it; some scenes are only peripherally related to this line, others intersect with the line at only one point. If we speak of the scenes as functional, they are functional not so much in the conventional dramatic sense, but in the way that parts of a poem are functional. The following scene, only slightly shorter than the average scene of the play, may serve as an example; it is set in Marie's room shortly before Woyzeck comes to murder her:

FOOL [*stretched out, telling fairy tales on his fingers*]: This one has a golden crown. He's Our Lord the King. Tomorrow I'll bring Her Royal Highness the Queen her child. . . . [Blood] Sausage says: come on, Liverwurst. . . .

MARIE [*leafing through the Bible*]: "And no guile is found in his mouth." Lord God, Lord God, don't look at me! [*Leafs again*] "And the scribes and the Pharisees brought unto him a woman taken in adultery, and set her in the midst . . . And Jesus said unto her, 'Neither do I condemn thee; go, and sin no more.'" Lord God, Lord God, I can't—Lord God, give me the strength to pray! [*The child cuddles up to her.*] The child stabs me to the heart. [*To the fool*] Karl! Strutting in the sun! [*The fool takes the child and becomes quiet.*] Franz hasn't been here yesterday or today. It's getting hot in here. [*She opens the window.*] "And stood at his feet weeping, and began to wash his feet with tears, and did wipe them with the hairs of her head, and kissed his feet, and anointed them with ointment." [*Beats her breast*] Everything's dead. Saviour, Saviour! If only I could anoint Thy feet!

The chief "function" of the scene is obviously to prepare for the murder scene by portraying Marie's uneasiness, while secondarily it attempts to "round out" Marie's character by demonstrating the guilt she feels at her faithlessness.

But such considerations, based as they are on traditional dramatic criticism, can only partly account for what Büchner is trying to say. One might ask, for instance, what the fool is doing here. Karl the fool, who appears in four scenes, has no practical function, unless one simply takes him to be a local idiot who happens to appear at various spots without explanation. His real function is much the same as that of the fool in *King Lear:* his fairy tale, like the ditties sung by Shakespeare's fool on the stormy heath, works as a kind of ironic counterpoint to Marie's expressions of guilt. (The fool in *Lear,* being on the king's payroll as a matter of course, had at least a more plausible practical function.) The fool's fairy tale, like the songs that appear throughout the play, is told only in fragments: Büchner, one might say, discovered what was not generally discovered until the time of the Symbolists—that fragments of statements can have a more powerful effect in an appropriate context than the statements in full.

In one sense the fool's fairy tale, with its lofty personages and its implied atmosphere of innocence, seems antithetical to Marie's statements of her guilt and fears. But the seemingly innocent name of a character, Blood Sausage, echoes a word in our mind which will re-echo again and again throughout the succeeding scenes. The words *red* and *blood* are firmly established for the audience long before the murder. "I smell blood," the fool, probably echoing a phrase from one of Grimm's fairy tales ("The Giant with the Three Golden Hairs"), had already told Woyzeck when the latter discovered Marie dancing with the drum major. The word *blood,* first associated with Marie's sensuality and sin—"She had a red, red mouth," Woyzeck had replied to the fool—only later comes to refer to the murder. "The moon's rising. It's red," Marie says to Woyzeck just before he draws his knife, while the latter replies, "Like a sword with blood on it!" After the murder, when blood is discovered on Woyzeck's hand while he is dancing at an inn, the fool takes up his tag once more, "And the Giant said: I smell, I smell. What do I smell? A man, a man who's bound for Hell! Pah! It stinks already!" Verbal patterns such as these, as Franz Mautner has shown in his study of the key words and images of *Woyzeck,*[1] are fundamental to Büchner's dramatic method in this play.

Marie's quotations from the Bible also serve as an indirect, though fairly obvious, means of extending the range of reference of the story Büchner is telling. He could not plausibly allow a simple girl like Marie to express her guilt with the eloquence of a Lady Macbeth; at the same time, if he had merely set down her anguished cries, without the intervening quotations, he might easily have committed a breach of dramatic tact. The quotations, one might note, are from three separate spots in the Bible: Marie could not possibly have come upon them accidentally. All are obviously relevant to her own situation. By interweaving them with her own words, Büchner creates a moment of almost unbearable pathos, climaxing as it does in her attempt to identify with Mary Magdalene. The *pastiche* method he employs is not present here, as it is elsewhere in the play, for ironic effect, but is a means of amplification, of setting what might have remained a simple domestic tragedy in a universal framework.

The fragments of songs which occur throughout the play also serve to create effects both of amplification and of ironic commentary on the action. Marie's longings for romance are obliquely suggested in an early scene when she sings a lullaby to her child about a gypsy who will lead him "straight into gypsyland." Woyzeck's expressions of jealousy are accompanied by the nonchalant singing of his friend Andres, who tells of a "merry maid" who "sits within her garden, / Till twelve o'clock has chimed away, / And the infantry comes mar-arching." In the scene just before the murder a chorus of girls sings a seemingly happy song, beginning:

The sun shines bright at Candlemas.
The corn is in full bloom.
They danced across the meadow grass,
They danced it two by two.

The reference to the dancing, however, reminds us of Marie and the drum major at the inn; indeed, the line with which Büchner breaks off the song, "Their stockings were the reddest red," calls to mind all the associations which the color *red* has accumulated up to this point. In the preceding scene, in fact, the color receives religious overtones, when Woyzeck remembers a verse written in his mother's Bible—

Lord, like Thy body, red and sore,
So let my heart be, evermore.

In one sense the songs serve to assert the folk-like character of the play, to remind us that the work is rooted "in the life of the very humblest person," as Büchner, by way of his character Lenz, had attempted to define the duty of the serious artist. In the same passage of Büchner's story—the discussion on aesthetics between Lenz, Kaufmann and Oberlin—Lenz had declared that "the sole criterion in matters of art" was "the feeling that there's life in the thing created. . . . We find such fullness of life . . . in Shakespeare; it strikes us with full impact in popular ballads and songs, only sometimes in Goethe."

And as Shakespeare and the early Goethe had done before him, Büchner liberally inserted ballads and songs in all his works. In *Danton's Death,* for instance, Lucille sings lines from a well-known folk song about the power of death just before her fatal cry, "Long live the king!" Rosetta in *Leonce and Lena* expresses her pain at Leonce's treatment of her in a song. Lenz, while preaching to Oberlin's congregation, is almost overcome with terror as he listens to a hymn about the need for the believer to experience Christ's sufferings. But nowhere in Büchner's work do songs appear with such profusion as in *Woyzeck*: fragments of thirteen different songs occur within the twenty-five pages which the text covers in the standard German edition. Indeed, as G.-L. Fink has pointed out in his exhaustive study of Büchner's use of songs, no serious German drama before *Woyzeck* shows them with such frequency.[2] Büchner drew his material from songs he had heard himself among the common people and from collections, above all, the collection of Alsatian songs compiled by his friends the Stöber brothers; although he is not known to have written any poems after his school-days, he may well have composed some of the songs for which no sources have yet been found. If the songs which fill the play serve in one sense to render that "fullness of life" which Büchner so evidently prizes, through the irony they express they work no less to evaluate and define the life which he attempted to record in the play. Their full symbolic possibilities may not even have occurred to Büchner when he started writing *Woyzeck:* through a study of the various manuscript versions Fink has shown that in the course of the play's composition the songs came to carry more and more symbolic weight and complexity.[3]

The type of complexity which Büchner achieved in *Woyzeck* is much the same as the kind which G. Wilson Knight discerned in Shakespeare when he spoke of the "spatial" composition which governs the major Shakespearean plays.[4] Thus the themes of *Hamlet* do not emerge simply through the temporal sequence of events, but through the atmosphere of corruption and decay suggested by songs, jokes, recurring words and images, and incidents seemingly irrelevant to the play's "main line" of action. Dramas essentially in the classical tradition—for instance Racine's or those of the mature Schiller—attempt to shape the temporal sequence of events in such a way that the play's central meanings and effects will emerge naturally from these events and their immediate reverberations; the fears and questionings voiced by a character such as Schiller's Wallenstein are a direct response to the events at each point of the play. *Danton's Death* breaks with this tradition to the extent that its meanings and effects emerge to a large degree from such apparent "side issues" as Danton's private contemplations, the hectic atmosphere of the Paris streets, and the contrasting modes of language in which characters such as Robespierre and Marion speak. In *Woyzeck* these side issues assume even larger proportions in relation to the "main action." A grandmother, for instance, appears from nowhere and tells a nihilistic fairy tale. An apprentice preaches a blasphemous sermon at an inn. Blood becomes a persistent word long before any real blood is dropped in the temporal sequence of events. Two carnival scenes, whose only connection with the "story" is that they provide a means for the drum major to notice Marie, contain the lengthy speeches of a charlatan showing off a monkey in costume and his wife in trousers, and of a concessionaire demonstrating the human skills of a trained horse.

One could speak of a kind of "dispersion" technique whereby the central themes are dispersed spatially within the speeches and songs of a large number of characters, many of whom have little or no connection with the temporal sequence. The real connection, for instance, between the carnival scenes and the rest of the play is a thematic one: the monkey, the horse, the wife in trousers are all in a sense "de-natured," perverted from their natural bent. One could, in fact, define most of the characters in the play through their varying relationships with nature, which, in the context that Büchner develops, itself becomes one of the key words of the play. The doctor, for example, not only attempts to control nature through his experiments, but chides Woyzeck mercilessly for the latter's inability to control his natural processes with his will. Woyzeck is paid by the doctor to maintain a diet of peas and to collect his urine for the doctor's experiments; but Woyzeck has proved unable to control his bladder. "I saw you, Woyzeck," the doctor scolds him. "You were pissing in the street. You were pissing against the wall, like a dog." To which Woyzeck can only reply, "But Doctor, when Nature calls." The doctor, however, is dissatisfied with such explanations: "When Nature calls! When Nature calls! Nature! Didn't I prove that the *musculus constrictor vesicae* can be controlled by the will? Woyzeck, Man is free!"

If the doctor is confident of man's ability to control nature, the captain shows a certain fear of natural processes and controls his impulses by convincing himself that he is governed by moral conventions: "Why, when I lie by my window after the rain and I see those white stockings flashing over the sidewalk—damn it, Woyzeck, then I know what love is too! I'm flesh and blood, too, Woyzeck. But virtue! Virtue! The things I could waste my time on! But I say to myself 'You're a virtuous man!' "

Compared to the doctor and captain, the lower-class characters remain their natural selves to a relatively high degree. But Büchner does not idealize their naturalness in any conventionally Rousseauistic way. Marie is a natural being in her spontaneousness and vitality, which show no trace of affectedness; yet her very naturalness makes possible the tragic consequences in which the drama culminates. The drum major stands at an opposite extreme from the captain and doctor: rather than denying or controlling his naturalness, he affects it to the point of perversity. "I'm a real man!" he loves to boast, pounding his chest at the same time. His seduction of Marie, though he flatters her by sending her earrings, is accomplished largely by a show

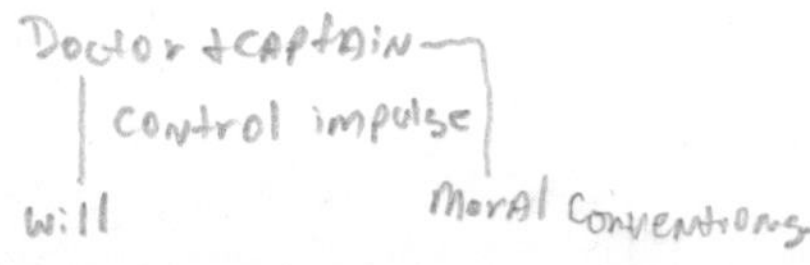

of animal forcefulness: "Let's raise a race of Drum-majors," he tells her as he embraces her.

Woyzeck's naturalness is less a positive attribute, as it is with Marie, than a reaction to the oppression to which he is subjected. He asserts his naturalness to the doctor only as a result of the absurd experiment which has been forced on him. His urinating against the wall is a reaction analogous to that shown by a cat which bites him as he picks it up after the doctor has thrown it out of a window. His strains of insanity, though Büchner attempts no direct diagnosis, could almost be interpreted as an involuntary immersion in a private world in response to the "unnatural" oppression from without. "When Nature gives way," he tells the doctor in an early draft, "the world gets dark and you have to feel around with your hands, and everything keeps slipping, like in a spider's web." He even speaks of a "double nature" which he has experienced—a condition in which "the sun stops at noon, and it's like the whole world's caught on fire."

The animals and the woman whom we see "de-natured," as it were, in the carnival scenes serve as analogies to the perverse relationships to nature which characters such as the captain, doctor, and drum major exemplify. The costumed monkey "walks upright, wears a fancy jacket and tight trousers, and carries a sword." "Look what Art has done for him!" the charlatan boasts. "He is no longer in the lowest ranks [of the human race]." Like the captain, the monkey (through his master's efforts, at least) has denied his basic nature. The horse, too, is described in human terms—"a member of all the learned societies, a professor here at our university, where he teaches the students to ride and to fence." He illustrates his ability at "double reasoning" by shaking his head, but soon after he is unexpectedly shown "mounting up indecently." Just as Woyzeck reacts to the doctor's oppression by urinating against a wall, so the horse openly asserts its natural self. Indeed, the concessionaire's excuse for the animal's behavior is almost a parody of Woyzeck's explanations for his "natural" acts: "This beast . . . is still in a state of nature. . . . Take a lesson from him. . . . Now, we have been told, be natural! You are created from dust, sand, and dung. Do you want to be more than dust, sand, and dung?"

It is basic to Büchner's technique in *Woyzeck* to approach a single theme from such varying points of view. The charlatan and concessionaire are themselves parodied in a later scene when the doctor asks Woyzeck to stand as a kind of exhibition before his students and demonstrate his ability to wiggle his ears: if the monkey and the horse were raised to human status, Woyzeck, in turn, is reduced to animal status. Büchner explores his characters' relationships to the natural order as a means of laying bare certain fundamental questions about the nature of being human. Are men essentially animals? Do they fool themselves in attributing a higher status to themselves than to animals? Do they perhaps not also fool themselves when they attempt to emulate animals? Like Shakespeare in his major tragedies, Büchner poses far more questions than he attempts to answer; his very technique, to the extent that his dramatic situations are re-examined in one analogous situation after another, eschews any air-tight answers.

Just as these dramatic situations are translated into different terms from one moment to the next, so individual words shift from one context to another. I noted earlier how the words *red* and *blood* accumulate associations in the course of the play. Even more fundamental to Büchner's central questions is the word *Mensch*—*man* or *human being*—and its derivative *menschlich*, which can mean both human and humane. From moment to moment throughout the play we hear this word slip from one of its meanings into another. The captain and the doctor, for instance, employ the word in its loftiest possible meaning—man as a free and autonomous being who is intrinsically superior to animals. "Der Mensch ist frei"—"Man is free. Through Man alone shines the individual's will to freedom!" the doctor declares as he chides Woyzeck for not controlling his bladder. As Wolfgang Martens has reminded us, the doctor's conception of man is stated essentially in the terms used by Kant and the idealist thinkers who followed him.[5]

The language he uses had become thoroughly stale by Büchner's time, and his declaration, given the context Büchner has placed it in, is obviously ridiculous. The captain works from the same conception when he prides himself alternately as a "virtuous man" and a "good man"—*ein tugendhafter Mensch, ein guter Mensch*—for his ability to resist sexual temptations. In the shaving scene, in which he employs the word *Mensch*—with one or the other of these adjectives—nine times, he contrasts himself with Woyzeck, who, because he has fathered an illegitimate child, by implication must be excluded from the honor of being a "human being." In the carnival scenes we note that the word *Mensch* need not be taken in such lofty terms: rather, being human is a matter of degree. The trained horse, for instance, is "ein tierischer Mensch"—a beastlike human being, and the monkey, costumed as a soldier, at least has a place on the "lowest step of the human race" (*menschliches Geschlecht*). The soldier-monkey, indeed, is an oblique analogy to the soldier Woyzeck, whose status on the chain of being—quite in contrast to those of the monkey and horse, who are given human attributes—is constantly lowered by the forces around him. By a terrible irony Woyzeck is finally honored with the designation *Mensch* as he drowns: two strangers, hearing anonymous sounds of gurgling from the pond, speculate that these are the sounds of a dying human being—"wie ein Mensch, der stirbt!"

It is the burden of the play to break down and expose those meanings of the word which can no longer hold up in the world which we see depicted here. In his mock sermon the apprentice attacks another of the word's "lofty" meanings—this one from a Biblical rather than a philosophical context—when he ironically intones, "What is Man? What is Man?" As he goes on, still employing Biblical language, he portrays man's purpose as a considerably less lofty one than the Bible does: "On what would the farmer, the cooper, the cobbler, and the doctor live—if God had not created Man?"

But the most forthright statements on man's precariousness and lowliness of status are left to Woyzeck himself, who experiences two moments of tragic recognition. When he discovers Marie's faithlessness, he makes one of the few serious general statements which are uttered in the play: "Jeder Mensch ist ein Abgrund"—"[Every man] is a precipice. You get dizzy when you look down." And shortly after, when he sees her dancing with the drum major, he recognizes the full animal-likeness of human behavior: "Male and Female! Man and Beast! They'll do it in broad daylight! They'll do it on your hands, like flies!" If the carnival scenes had overestimated the human qualities of beasts, and if the doctor's experiments had worked to reduce man to animal status, Marie's faithlessness simply demonstrates the basic equivalence of man and beast. Marie, at least, never attempts to idealize the nature of mankind: when she says to herself at one point, "Ich bin doch ein schlecht Mensch," she is using the word *Mensch* in the neuter gender, where it means "loose woman"—"I'm [a vile whore after all.] I could stab myself." For her and for Woyzeck the word has been stripped of its more elevated trappings. Not that Büchner has any final definitions of the word to offer; he merely presents it to us in all its various shades of meaning and lets us measure these meanings against the dramatic context.

It goes without saying that no translation could ever do justice to a text which reveals its essential meanings to such a degree through individual words. An English translator, for instance, is forced to employ a whole variety of words to render the meanings of *Mensch*. Because so much of its power depends on the force of key words and also on the folklike quality of its songs and dialogue, *Woyzeck* is doubtless the hardest to translate of Büchner's works. Yet by the same token it is also his most evocative, and through its immense concentration and its terseness of manner, his most explosive.

ii

Like much of the best realist art of the nineteenth century *Woyzeck* is based on a real person and a real incident. The realist imagination was often fed by seemingly trivial local incidents—one need only mention Stendhal's transformation of Antoine Berthet into Julien Sorel, or Flaubert's use of gossip about the adulterous daughter-in-law of one of his mother's friends. The real Woyzeck had been executed in Leipzig in 1824 for murdering his mistress. His case had aroused considerable attention, not only because it was Leipzig's first public execution in thirty years, but principally because Woyzeck's probable insanity raised some doubts as to whether justice was properly done. Soon after his death the case was re-examined and, as a result of testimony by a prominent Leipzig physician named Clarus, the original verdict was substantiated. The case was not quite forgotten, however, and a decade later was reopened once more: Woyzeck was found of unsound mind, and exonerated. The basic humanitarian questions which the case by its very nature raised doubtless helped shape the material in his mind. But the immediate source for the drama was Clarus' report, which Büchner probably found in the medical journals which his father collected.[6]

The Clarus report approaches Woyzeck from a rigidly moralistic point of view very close in spirit to that of the captain in Büchner's play: "The only motive for the crime," Clarus smugly closes his report, "was the preponderance of passion over reason." [7] Yet, as with *Danton's Death* and *Lenz*, Büchner drew innumerable details from his source. Woyzeck's apocalyptic visions, his irrational fears of freemasons, his background as barber and soldier, his discovery of his mistress dancing with another man at an inn—all these were present in Clarus' report. Even some of the key words and phrases which go through the play were suggested by the report, for instance, the virtually untranslatable phrase "immer zu"—"roll on," "let it happen," "always"—which Marie mutters as she dances and which haunts Woyzeck's mind throughout the rest of the play.

But Büchner also introduced some significant changes. The original Marie, one Frau Woost, was neither young nor attractive, but a widow of forty-six, five years older than

Woyzeck (whose middle name, Christian, Büchner changed first to Louis, then to Franz). Without idealizing them in any way, Büchner attempted to make both Woyzeck and Marie more dignified and more appealing than their originals. Frau Woost, for instance, had been suspected of loose behavior with a number of other men and had borne Woyzeck no children, while he, in turn, had had an illegitimate child by an earlier mistress, and in a still earlier relationship had threatened to kill a mistress on account of her faithlessness. In the play, we are given the impression that Woyzeck's relationship to Marie, quite in contrast to that of his model, is essentially a marriage, even if without sanction of clergy, and that her seduction by the drum major, though a natural consequence of her character, was no casual event for her.

Significantly, Büchner chose not to send his hero to his execution: the oppression to which he is subjected by the world around him is punishment enough. But the precise ending which he intended to give the play still remains uncertain. There seems no doubt any longer that Woyzeck is meant to drown in the pond as he hides the knife (whether he is a suicide is not altogether certain); for many years, however, through a misinterpretation of the role of a minor character in Büchner's early drafts for the play, it was thought that Büchner, had he completed the fragment, would have seen Woyzeck through his trial and execution.[8]

The major uncertainties that still underlie the text have to do with the exact order of the scenes. There is no reason to believe that Büchner intended to add any scenes to those left in the manuscript, but he doubtless intended to subject some to revision. The manuscripts which Franzos found consist of two early drafts, each of different segments of the play, together with a sheet of extra scenes and what seems a fair-copy revision of most of the play. This fair copy, which includes some scenes not found in the earlier drafts, unfortunately leaves off before the murder scene. As a result, Büchner's editors have had to piece together the last scenes from the various early drafts. Indeed, every edition and translation must represent each man's interpretation of Büchner's final intentions. The now outmoded Franzos edition—as well as Alban Berg's opera, which was based on it and which also retains Franzos' misreading of the hero's name as Wozzeck—quite willfully fuses together two scenes which were difficult to accommodate in the text separately, but which have no real relationship to one another. The resulting scene, in which a group of children go out to view Marie's body and which ends with Marie's child on his hobbyhorse, provided Berg with a highly effective ending for the opera. The well-known Hoffman English translation retains this scene, though, like the Franzos text, it adds still another scene, consisting of only a single speech, as an ending. The speech is that of a policeman investigating the murder: "A real murder, a first-rate murder, a beautiful murder. As beautiful a little murder as you could ask for. It's a long time since we had one like this." I, for one, have always felt uncomfortable with this scene, for the crudeness of its irony seems to me out of keeping with the tone of the other later scenes of the play; moreover, drawn as it is from an early draft, it need carry no more authority than other scenes from these drafts which editors have chosen to eliminate.

Among the scenes which do not usually find their way into editions (except in the critical apparatus, if any is provided), the two scenes which Franzos rewrote and fused together should, I think, be restored to the text in their original condition. The first of these would seem to belong between the murder scene and the scene in which Woyzeck is dancing at the inn. It depicts Woyzeck coming to see his child after the murder:

KARL [*holding the child on his lap*]: This one fell in the water, this one fell in the water, this one fell in the water.

WOYZECK Christian!

KARL [*looking fixedly at him*]: This one fell in the water.

WOYZECK [*trying to embrace the child, who turns away and screams*]: God!

KARL This one fell in the water.

WOYZECK Christian, I'll buy you a hobby-horse [*the child resists him*] [*to Karl*] Go buy the kid a hobby-horse!

[*Karl looks at him fixedly*]

WOYZECK Giddyap, giddyap, horsy!

KARL [*shouting with joy*]: Giddyap, giddyap! Horsy, horsy! [*runs off with the child*]

The scene represents the final and in some ways most painful rejection to which Woyzeck is subjected—rejection by his own child. The fool's song—the first line of an Alsatian children's rhyme—works contrapuntally against Woyzeck's efforts to make contact with the child: it guards against sentiment, as it were, while at the time increasing the pathos immeasurably. The final irony is that only the fool, and not the child, can work up any enthusiasm about the hobbyhorse. Obliquely the song may perhaps re-echo in our minds once more several scenes later as Woyzeck is drowning. Indeed, its reference to falling in the water is probably the main reason that editors have excluded the scene: taking the fool's words literally (even though he is never to be taken literally elsewhere in the play), many must have thought these words refer directly to Woyzeck, who, coming home wet after hiding his knife, would thus never have drowned at all.

The other scene which I think deserves to be restored in its untampered state is that of the children playing:

FIRST CHILD Let's get Marie!

SECOND CHILD What for?

FIRST CHILD Don't you know? Everybody's gone out there. There's a dead woman there!

SECOND CHILD Where?

FIRST CHILD To the left past the pond in the forest, near the red cross.

SECOND CHILD Hurry up so we can still see something before they bring her back.

The children's curiosity, combined as it is with a kind of natural, childlike callousness toward death, provides still another perspective on the questions about human dignity which have been posed throughout the play. In the manuscripts this scene is placed between the scene at the inn and Woyzeck's drowning, and there is no reason, I think, that it should not be retained there.

As for the ending, if the manuscripts contain all the scenes which Büchner intended to utilize in his final draft—and this may well be the case—the drowning, followed as it is in most editions with the voices of two persons who are about to discover Woyzeck's body, provides as appropriate a conclusion as any.[9] The eerieness of the atmosphere—"So foggy, that gray mist everywhere, and the bugs humming like broken bells"—dissolves the drama in a world of unreality which has been hovering at its edges from the start. The inconclusiveness (in the traditional dramatic sense) of this ending is as fitting to the play as the deliberate inconclusiveness of the much-praised hobby-horse scene with which Berg concludes the opera but which could not possibly follow Büchner's intentions.

Not only the final scenes, but also a number of early ones could easily have been meant to follow a different sequence from that of standard editions. For instance, the decision of most editors to open the play with Woyzeck shaving the captain is a quite arbitrary one, since in the fair copy this scene appears much later, between the first and second scenes in Marie's room. Büchner's editors have doubtless been motivated by the fact that the shaving scene provides a good deal of "exposition" about Woyzeck's domestic situation. The fair copy (which need not, however, be taken as a final authority) begins with what is usually printed as the second scene, in which Woyzeck and Andres are gathering wood. One wonders if this scene, with its weird background effects suggested by Woyzeck's visions, might not provide a more suitable opening. From a conventional dramatic point of view the scene is undoubtedly more "confusing" than the shaving scene, in which the hero seems relatively clearheaded and thus has much expository information to offer the audience. But *Woyzeck* is no conventional drama, and there is no reason that its scenes be arranged to fit conventional notions about drama. Büchner's technique of developing his themes by analogy and parody, and of dispersing some of his most meaningful images and situations outside the central "plot line" surely must be taken into account by any editor or director trying to reconstitute the order of scenes as Büchner intended it. In the light of the searching studies that have been made of the play in recent years, it would seem appropriate to reopen the whole manuscript problem to bring future texts of the play in line with what we now know of Büchner's dramaturgy.

iii

In *Woyzeck* one can distinguish two approaches to character. The first approach is perhaps most notably exemplified in Büchner's depiction of Marie. Marie is an "objectively" created character, like Marion and most of the other characters of *Danton's Death*. Büchner gives us the illusion of a being who exists independently of her author. She is simply *there*; no judgment is passed on her, either directly or implicitly. She reveals herself through the immediacy of her speech and her actions. Through the subtlety and fullness with which she is presented, Büchner's portrait of Marie exemplifies the type of realist art which he must have had in mind in the words spoken by Lenz to Oberlin and Kaufmann: "If only artists would try to submerge themselves in the life of the very humblest person and to reproduce it with all its faint agitations, hints of experience, the subtle, hardly perceptible play of his features." It is remarkable, indeed, how fully rounded Büchner's portrait of her is, for she doubtless appears on-stage for less time than any other heroine in a major drama. A whole aspect of her character is often presented in a single gesture or sentence—her exuberance, for instance, when she tries on her new earrings before her mirror; her animal vitality in the seduction scene; her tenderness while she sings her child to sleep; her uncontrolled anguish in the Bible scene; her straightforward earthiness when she talks back to her prying neighbor; her pride when Woyzeck attempts to hit her ("Just touch me, Franz! I'd rather have a knife in my ribs than your hands on me. At ten, my father didn't dare touch me."). Through her humble background and her naturalness she inevitably recalls Gretchen in Goethe's *Faust,* as almost every commentator on the play has had occasion to observe. Not only is her scene at the mirror an obvious echo of Gretchen's jewel scene, but in an early draft of *Woyzeck* she even had the same name (or rather Margreth, of which Gretchen is a diminutive). Yet the uninhibitedness with which Büchner records her and her world gives her a far greater degree of earthiness than one finds among even the humblest characters in *Faust.*

Although the lower-class characters of Büchner's play are not presented as fully as Woyzeck and Marie, they are conceived with the same dramatic objectivity which I have described above. It is a sign of this objectivity that they often speak in dialect—or, to be precise, in an unsystematic blend of the Hessian and Alsatian dialects which Büchner heard from the people among whom he lived.[10] Their speech is racy and is spoken so naturally that the symbolism which lurks beneath the surface is totally unobtrusive. But the captain and the doctor were created in an entirely different manner from that of the lower-class characters. Quite in contrast to the latter, they have no autonomy of their own; as Wolfgang Kayser has put it, they are essentially marionettes, totally at the mercy of the various fixed ideas which motivate all their behavior.[11] When they confront each other on the street, for example, they seem wholly stylized as characters:

DOCTOR [*showing him his hat*] Do you know who that is, Captain? That's Mr. Emptyhead, my dear Drill-killer.
CAPTAIN [*showing a button hole*] Do you know who this is, Doctor? That's Mr. Hole-in-the-Head, my dear Coffin-nail.

Their comic routine at this point could easily be out of a vaudeville act. Rather than real characters, they are essentially caricatures. The doctor and captain are by far the most talkative characters in the play, yet the talk they engage in does not serve to round them out or to reveal new facets of their personalities; rather, their talk merely heaps up the same kind of details in endless succession. The doctor's whole being is dependent on his experiments; when he starts talking he loses track of all other aspects of reality:

> Pissing against a wall! Tsk, tsk, tsk! I have it in writing, the agreement's right here. And what do I see? With my own eyes I saw it. I stick my nose out the window, letting the sun's rays hit it to observe the process of sneezing, and what do I see? . . . [*Bearing down on Woyzeck*] No, Woyzeck, I'm not getting angry. Anger is unhealthy, it's unscientific. I'm calm, perfectly calm. My pulse is beating its regular 60, and I'm addressing you in an absolutely cold-blooded manner. Why get angry with a [human being], God forbid! A [mere human being]! Now if [it were a Proteus that went wrong] . . . But, Woyzeck, you shouldn't have been pissing against that wall.

Through the force of his fixed idea the doctor has dehumanized himself to the point where he dare not show anger ("it's unscientific"), even when the success of his experiments is threatened. He is not so much addressing Woyzeck as talking to himself; he has no inkling, in fact, of any world which exists outside his own. The total impression he leaves as a result of all such details which pile up in his speeches is that of a grotesque being of almost monstrous proportions.

Büchner had occasionally employed caricature in his earlier work, for instance in the bombastic stage-prompter Simon in *Danton's Death*, or in the metaphysically confused King Peter in *Leonce and Lena*. But nowhere does it assume the dimensions which it does in *Woyzeck*. The doctor and the captain, after all, are the only representatives in the drama of the ruling class which is oppressing Woyzeck. By portraying them in grotesque terms Büchner is able to demonstrate both the absurdity and the horror of their world at the same time. Moreover, by confronting a caricature like the doctor with a "realistically" conceived character like Woyzeck, Büchner was able to achieve a unique blend of comedy and pathos different in its effect from anything in his earlier heroes. Note, for instance, the scene in which Woyzeck is put on exhibit for the doctor's students:

DOCTOR Just look at this man. For three months, he's eaten nothing but peas. Note the result. Just feel him! What an irregular pulse. And those eyes!

WOYZECK Everything's getting black, Doctor. [*He sits down.*]

DOCTOR Courage, Woyzeck! A couple of days and it will be over. Feel that pulse, gentlemen, feel it. [*The students fumble over his pulse, temples, and chest.*] Incidentally, Woyzeck, wiggle your ears for the gentlemen. I've been intending to show you this. He does it with two muscles. Come on, snap into it!

WOYZECK Doctor! Oh!

Woyzeck is realistically enough conceived so that we sympathize with him, in fact to some degree identify with him. But as the doctor draws him into his orbit and overpowers him, Woyzeck, too, comes to seem absurd. Yet however great his absurdity, we continue to sympathize with him as with a real human being ("Everything's getting black, Doctor"). He is perhaps the first tragic hero whom we can laugh at and pity at once.

Attacks on the pretensions of doctors and scientists were nothing new in literature by Büchner's time—one thinks immediately of Molière's absurd physicians or of an irresponsible scientist like Mary Shelley's Frankenstein. But Büchner's doctor is presented with a degree of concreteness which may well be something new in the history of the doctor motif in literature. Not that we can describe him as essentially a modern scientist: his "science" is still hopelessly tied to German idealist philosophy, as we note when he attempts to lecture to his students about "the important problem of the relation between the subject and the object." But in his zeal to perform "the most immortal experiments," as he puts it at one point, and to perform them at whatever the human cost, he demonstrates a kind of *hybris* which bears no trace of Faustian glory and is at once as frightening as it is absurd.

It seems appropriate that this attack on the pretensions

of science should come from a writer who was himself a trained and dedicated scientist. Büchner, in fact, found his material very close at hand, for his doctor is essentially a portrait of one of his professors at Giessen, J. B. Wilbrand, who himself used to stage the ear-wiggling demonstration with his son in Woyzeck's role; Wilbrand's own writings, at least those excerpts which a Büchner scholar has reprinted, are not only strikingly similar to lines spoken by the doctor in the play, but they also sound like an unintentional self-parody.[12] One might note that Büchner's own students remembered his class lectures at Zurich for their sober concreteness and their scrupulous refusal to indulge in rhetorical ornamentation and the various rhetorical excesses which many scientists of his time had borrowed from the German idealist philosophers.[13]

Although Büchner's caricature of the doctor is aimed directly at his conduct as a professional man—the doctor, in fact, is totally defined by his professionalism—his portrait of the captain has no connection with the latter's professional attributes. The captain, indeed, is about as far removed as possible from the traditional *miles gloriosus*. "A good man doesn't have courage!" the captain says in an early draft. "A mongrel bitch has courage! I went to war only to strengthen my love of life." The center of Büchner's portrait of the captain lies not in his actions—he is a totally passive character—but in his moralizing and his introspection. His most frequent words are *virtuous* and *good;* much of the grotesqueness we feel about him derives from the repetitiveness with which he keeps using the same clichés: "A good man doesn't look moody." "A good man is someone with a good conscience." "Woyzeck, you're a good man, but you have no morals." "Woyzeck, you have no virtue." "A good man, with a clear conscience, doesn't run so fast." Through his empty moralizing, as Martens has suggested in his essay on the captain, he is a parody not of a soldier, but of a stupid provincial bourgeois, with distinct affinities to such a figure as Flaubert's M. Homais.[14]

Yet the captain's personality also encompasses one area

which is notably lacking in Homais and his successors in drama and fiction. For the captain is the only spokesman in the play for the horrors of boredom. "You'll finish up early," he says apprehensively to Woyzeck while the latter is shaving him, "and what'll I do with ten minutes on my hands?" In Büchner's earlier works such sentiments were expressed only by his heroes, and as such we were meant to treat them with a certain degree of sympathy. Woyzeck and his class have little leisure for ennui and could scarcely have embodied this persistent Büchner theme. But the captain's ennui gains none of our sympathy; it is every bit as ridiculous as his pronouncements on moral conduct. The melancholy he complains of has neither Danton's fortitude and self-knowledge to back it, nor has it Lenz' visionary grandeur. It strikes us, instead, as embarrassingly sentimental: "Doctor, I'm feeling [depressed, I'm emotionally wrought up (*schwärmerisch*). . . . I start crying whenever I see my coat hanging on the wall.]" His dizzy spells and irrational fears are a kind of comic analogy to Woyzeck's irrational symptoms; like Woyzeck, too, he is an object of the doctor's mania for experiments. Yet it is also significant that Büchner chose to stress the captain's inward instability: the oppression and the callousness of which Woyzeck is a victim are thus themselves shown as products of a sick and precarious world.

iv

In the character of Woyzeck Büchner would seem to have carried the idea of a passive hero about as far as it can possibly go. For Woyzeck is victimized in every conceivable way—by his poverty, his social degradation, his mistress' faithlessness, his rival's brutality, and his frightening mental visions. Even his companion Andres, uncomprehending and insensitive, is almost a parody of a dramatic *confident*. Yet by a kind of paradox Woyzeck is the only one of Büchner's heroes who ends up by actively asserting himself: his murder of Marie, in its premeditatedness and brutality, and his subsequent suicide are as extreme a form of self-assertion as his earlier subservience to the forces around him was an extreme form of passivity. Büchner has seen clearly that the ultimate result of oppression is rebellion on the part of the victim; Woyzeck's affinities among Büchner's earlier heroes are not with Danton or Leonce, but with the mad Lucille shouting "Long live the king!" or the mad Lenz in his violent moments of jumping out windows. From our mid-twentieth-century vantage point, Woyzeck seems a more approachable tragic hero than the standard Aristotelian model; in an impersonal world that lacks a commonly shared set of values we are less likely to feel fear and terror at the fall of a great personage than at the violent self-assertion of an underdog hero who rebels against his fate after the most outrageous provocation. Woyzeck's rebellion is as natural and instinctive as the two analogies which Büchner draws from the natural order: a cat that bites back after being thrown out the window and a horse that "mounts up indecently" when it is forced to play a human role.

As an image of the eternal victim, Woyzeck, somewhat surprisingly, never indulges in self-pity. At times, indeed, one discerns a certain measure of humor with which he contemplates the hopelessness of his condition. "If we ever did get into heaven, they'd put us to work on the thunder," he tells the captain when the latter chides him for the "immorality" of his domestic situation. His method of defending himself against the doctor ("But, Doctor, when Nature calls . . ."), despite the cruelty we feel in the doctor's treatment of him, has an indubitably comic effect for us. To the degree that he is continually beaten down he has something of the eternal clown about him. "One thing after the other," he says resignedly after the drunken drum major has given him a beating; though we are scarcely tempted to laugh at this point, the clownlike resignation of his remark works to hold back any feelings of pity we might be tempted to indulge on him. Büchner early discovered what such later creators of downtrodden heroes as Charlie Chaplin and Samuel Beckett were to find fundamental to their art: that an audience's sympathy for the hero could only be sustained by means of comic devices which would prevent them from showering pity on him.

Despite his clownlike moments, there are times in the play when Woyzeck seems invested with some of the articulateness and dignity traditional to a tragic hero. His statement to Andres in the barracks, "You know, Andres, she was one girl in a thousand" (only an approximate rendering of the untranslatable "Aber, Andres, sie war doch ein einzig Mädel") is memorable as one of his few truly reflective moments in the play. Although Marie is still alive at this point, Woyzeck's use of the past tense suggests that he has already determined his course of action. We feel a special poignancy through the combination of this past tense with the tender attitude which the sentence as a whole expresses toward Marie; the poignancy, indeed, is increased by Andres' inability to figure out whom Woyzeck is talking about. "Who was?" he asks blankly, to which Woyzeck, reduced to isolation as always, replies, "Never mind. So long."

There is one scene, just before the murder, in which Woyzeck betrays a calmness and clarity evident nowhere else in the play. He rummages among his belongings in the barracks and presents Andres with a jacket plus a cross and a ring which had belonged to his sister; then he pulls out a sacred picture which had been in his mother's Bible. It is significant that this scene does not appear in any of the extant early drafts, but only in the fair-copy revision, of which it is, in fact, the last scene before this manuscript breaks off: for Büchner may well have felt the need to remind the audience that Woyzeck, for all his mental aberrations and his isolation from the human community, shares at least a human past with it. Family memories which might have seemed sentimental in another context work here to endow Woyzeck with the basic human dignity which we have seen him systematically deprived of in earlier scenes. The most moving passage of this scene occurs when he reads aloud from his military identification document: "Private Friedrich Johann Franz Woyzeck, Rifleman, 2nd Regiment, 2nd Battalion, Company

Four. Born Feast of the Annunciation, July 20th. I'm thirty years, seven months, and twelve days old." For the hitherto passive Woyzeck this simple recital of vital statistics serves as an assertion of self-identity: if he is nothing else in the grotesque world with which Büchner has surrounded him he can at least lay claim to being a statistical entity.

Like Lenz, Woyzeck could be looked upon as "half mad," close enough to the normal world of the audience to make contact with it, yet also prey to a private world which sometimes threatens to engulf him from within. And as with Lenz, his mental condition as it is depicted in the play can be looked at in two ways—as a record of a clinical fact, and as a means of portraying far greater imaginative resources within him than a naturalistic portrait of a man of his background could provide. The images of Woyzeck's visions are drawn largely from the Bible, and most particularly from Revelation:

> Andres, look how bright it is. It's all shiny over the city. There's a fire running around the sky, and a sound coming down like trumpets. It's closing in on us!
>
> * * *
>
> Marie, it happened again. Plenty. Doesn't the good book say, "And behold, there was a smoke coming up from the land like the smoke of an oven"?

Similarly to the scene in which Marie identifies herself with Mary Magdalene, these passages testify to Büchner's recognition that the narrow world of people like Woyzeck and Marie has at least the Bible to provide it with larger imaginative perspectives. Indeed, as a result of the imaginative capacity which Woyzeck has shown in his feverish visions throughout the play, he is able to articulate his tragic burden with the inward intensity which earlier, more elevated tragic heroes had been able to display. His agonized and frantic monologue after the scene in which he sees Marie and the drum major dancing shares something of the intensity of Lear's scene on the heath:

> Don't stop! Don't stop! Hish! Hash! That's the way the flutes and fiddles go. Don't stop! Don't stop! No more

music! Who's talking under there? [*He stretches out on the ground*] What? What are you saying? Louder! Louder! Stab, stab the bitch of a goat-wolf dead? Stab, stab the bitch of a goat-wolf dead! Should I? Must I? Is it out there, too? Is the wind saying it, too? The words don't stop! Don't stop! Stab her dead! Dead!

The powerful imaginative structure which Büchner has created in this speech fuses together such diverse components as Marie's words at the dance, "*immer zu*," rendered here as "Don't stop," nonsense words like "Hish! Hash!," the sound of the wind, and the mysterious voices which have been haunting him throughout the play. Translation can give at best a rough equivalent of this passage, for Büchner depends above all on evocative sound combinations and repetitions for his effects here. The phrase "bitch of a goat-wolf" is in fact no translation at all, for Büchner's word, "*Zickwolfin*," is not a recognizable word, though through its auditory connotations, as Margaret Jacobs has shown in her detailed discussion of the etymological backgrounds of the word, it may suggest a "rapacious she-wolf."[15] Büchner was doubtless struck by the auditory possibilities suggested by a phrase in Clarus' medical report, "Stich die Frau Woostin tot!"—"Stab Mrs. Woost dead!"—which the real-life Woyzeck claimed to have heard from his voices.[16] The distance between the almost ludicrous phrase in the medical report and its frighteningly evocative counterpart in the monologue suggests the distance which separates the material with which Büchner started from the work of art he wrought out of it; despite its uniqueness in the history of dramatic literature, in its most agitated moments it succeeds in renewing something of the lofty tone which we associate with the great tragic dramas of the past.

v

Woyzeck's own words to the captain provide the groundwork for any sociological interpretation of the play which one might wish to develop: "You see, Captain—with us poor people—it's money, money! If you don't have money . . . Well, you just can't have morals when you're bringing someone like yourself into the world. We're only flesh and blood. People like us can't be holy in this world—or the next. If we ever did get into heaven, they'd put us to work on the thunder."

In confounding the captain's insensitive use of the word *morals*, Woyzeck not only suggests an economic basis for his dilemma—"it's money, money"—but voices a notion that was to become a major premise of nineteenth-century social thought—that one's moral habits are shaped by, and relative to, the economic and social environment. As long as one is content with a superficial reading of the play, one could interpret Woyzeck and Marie's tragedy in terms of this remark. The play would thus emerge as a violent protest against the economic and social oppression to which the lower classes are subjected; the very grotesqueness with which the doctor and the captain—the two representatives in the play of the ruling class—are depicted, would indicate the intensity with which Büchner voices his protest. Indeed, from all we know about Büchner the man—the fact that he addressed the *Hessian Messenger* not to the middle class but directly to the poor; his statement in a letter, even after his revolutionary career was concluded, that "the only revolutionary element in the world is the relation between rich and poor" (and not, as others of his time thought, the opposition between liberals and absolutists)[17]—the play *Woyzeck* would seem to invite interpretation as a social document.

And to a certain degree, surely, it does. There are doubtless few earlier literary works of comparable stature which treat lower-class life as intimately and sympathetically and with as little condescension. The play includes enough elements of revolutionary sentiment—the squalor with which the life of the poor is depicted, the arrogance of the ruling class, the crude economic interpretation of religion in the apprentice's sermon—that an undiscerning audience might easily pigeonhole it among the Naturalist plays of the turn of the century or the proletarian dramas written between the last two wars.

But *Woyzeck* is obviously something more than a protest against social injustice, it is a violent protest against the universe itself. The conditions which we see leading to Woyzeck's crime cannot be explained simply by the social and economic pressures which have shaped him; rather, they seem inherent in the life-process—in Marie's human weakness, in the visions that oppress Woyzeck from within, in the unnaturalness of the atmosphere which permeates the play. As Kurt May has reminded us, not a line in the play voices any real hope for social change.[18] Nor is there any real villain whom one can consistently point to—neither the drum major, who is no easy object of blame like the seducer figure in Victorian melodrama, nor the captain and doctor, who, unsavory as they are, play no direct role in Woyzeck's crime except to arouse his suspicions of the drum major. The very fact that Büchner does not draw direct connections between the murder and the evils to which Woyzeck is subjected is a sign that these evils are generally dispersed within the world out of which the play is built. The fairy tale which the grandmother tells just before the murder is a kind of parable on the nature of this world:

> Once upon a time there was a poor little girl who had no father or mother because everyone was dead and there was no one left in the whole world. Everyone was dead, and she went off and kept looking for someone night and day. And since there was no one on earth, she thought she'd go to heaven. The moon looked out at her so friendly, but when she finally got to it, it was just a piece of rotted wood. So she went on to the sun, and when she got there, it was just a dried up sunflower. And when she got to the stars, they were just little gold flies stuck up there as if they'd been caught in a spider web. And when she thought she'd go back to earth, it was just an upside down pot. And she was all alone. And so she sat down and cried. And she's still sitting there, all alone.

Büchner's idea of embodying this story in a fairy tale is as bold an inversion of genre convention as the content of the tale is an inversion of our common-sense notions of reality. As in *Danton's Death*, the image of the world we are shown in *Woyzeck* is a world upside down ("when she thought she'd go back to earth, it was just an upside down pot"). In *Danton's Death,* however, Büchner had at hand a ready-made image of an inverted world—an image, moreover, which an audience could immediately recognize as historically authentic. In *Woyzeck* he was forced to create this image by more indirect means—by his sustained man-animal analogies, by grotesquely ridiculous scenes such as Woyzeck's ear-wiggling exhibition, by Woyzeck's oppressive Biblical visions, by occasional images of a distinctly surrealistic character ("The moon's . . . like a sword with blood on it," "bugs humming like broken bells").

But the fairy tale offers perhaps too simple an analogy to the world portrayed in the play; like all parables, it oversimplifies to make its point. The world we actually experience in the play is never defined for us in any one statement. The song fragments, the cryptic remarks of the fool, the Biblical quotations—all, whatever their obvious dramatic functions, help suggest more distant perspectives which no single thesis about the play, sociological or otherwise, could conceivably exhaust. As in much modern poetry—for example, Eliot's *The Waste Land* or Georg Trakl's lyrics—the fragmentary statements and the incongruous juxtapositions help create an illusion of mystery and unreality. With *Woyzeck*—in contrast to *Danton's Death*—we should speak not so much of a world upside down as of a world in dissolution. Yet behind this sense of unreality one fact emerges insistently throughout the play—the reality and horror of human suffering. Woyzeck's passive suffering provides the modern mind with an image which, through its grimness and power, in the final analysis silences all questions about its origins and its ultimate meanings.

6 FOREBEARS, DESCENDANTS, AND CONTEMPORARY KIN: BÜCHNER AND LITERARY TRADITION

BÜCHNER'S REVOLT against a classicism gone stale was by no means the first such revolt in German drama. The Storm-and-Stress writers of the 1770's, in the name of spontaneity and truthfulness to nature, and with Lessing's criticism and Shakespeare's example to back them, had succeeded in clearing the German stage of its dreary, "correct" neo-classical drama—a development of the mid-eighteenth century which, as we now see it, never produced anything of lasting value anyway and whose best-known work, Gottsched's *Dying Cato* (1730), is nothing more than a pale, academic imitation of French and English plays on the same theme. One can, indeed, look at the history of German drama as a kind of alternation between relatively tight "classical" forms of one sort or another, and looser forms which derive much of their energy from their conscious revolt against an out-going theatrical tradition. Bertolt Brecht's demand for an "epic theater" can be interpreted as the latest of a number of war cries which have resounded in German dramatic criticism at various times in the last two hundred years.

Büchner's work bears only superficial resemblances to the major single achievement of the Storm-and-Stress drama, Goethe's *Götz von Berlichingen* (1773). Like *Danton's Death, Götz* presents a vast historical panorama composed of short, loosely connected scenes. Through their common attempt to render what they saw as Shakespeare's truthfulness to nature, both writers achieved a fullness and earthiness of detail and created a multitude of characters who seem to breathe with a life of their own. Yet two works could scarcely be more different in spirit than *Götz* and *Danton's Death,* for Goethe's play above all demonstrates the possibility of heroic action and meaningful human relationships—the very values toward which Büchner's work expresses the most uncompromising skepticism.

But there was one dramatist of the '70's for whom Büchner felt a fundamental affinity, and that was Lenz. Büchner was drawn to Lenz not only through the personal sympathy he obviously felt toward him, but also through his interest in his plays, especially *The Private Tutor* (1774) and *The Soldiers* (1776), which he mentions in his story on Lenz. These two plays are essentially like miniature paintings, if I may borrow a term which Brecht applied to *The Private Tutor,* a play he adapted for his Berlin Ensemble.[1] In their fusion of comic and tragic moods, in their uncondescending representation of ordinary people, above all, in the concreteness and fullness with which they depict a contemporary environment, they look forward to *Woyzeck* more than any other works in earlier German drama. In his slightly ridiculous, pathetic heroes—the young cloth merchant Stolzius in *The Soldiers,* the private tutor Läuffer—Lenz presents a type of passive hero which Büchner could later develop in the character of Woyzeck. Like Büchner, Lenz allows his characters to reveal themselves through their peculiarities of language; within a single play, in fact, he presents a generous selection of human beings, each asserting his individuality by his manner of speech. Lenz' characters often seem sharply individualized in the way Büchner suggested through the words he put into Lenz' mouth: "If only artists would try to submerge themselves in the life of the very humblest person and to reproduce it with all its faint agitations, hints of experience, the subtle, hardly perceptible play of his features." [2]

The discussion of aesthetics in Büchner's story, partly drawn as it is from Lenz' own critical pronouncements, provides some clues to the aims the two writers hold in common. Among other things, the discussion stresses the dignity and the poetry inherent in the lives of ordinary people. Speaking of the characters he had tried to create in *The Private Tutor* and *The Soldiers*, Büchner's Lenz calls them "the most prosaic people in the world, but the emotional vein is identical in almost every individual; all that varies is the thickness of the shell which this vein must penetrate." For the artist to capture the individuality of every being, he cannot create his characters according to conventional "types" or preconceived molds of any sort, but must observe concretely, indeed, "submerge himself" as he puts it, in his individual characters. The doctrine of realism which Büchner propounds is something far removed from the much more "scientific" doctrines of many writers in the later nineteenth century. For instance, Büchner's Lenz finds an attitude of love prerequisite to all successful artistic creation: "One must love human nature in order to penetrate into the peculiar character of any individual; nobody, however insignificant, however ugly, should be despised; only then can one understand human kind as a whole." By what seems a kind of paradox, a writer can create a world of autonomous human beings only through the love he feels for them; as soon as he begins to despise them, his characters lose their individuality and become mere puppets. The artist, in fact, plays a role analogous to God's, both in the plenitude and the variety with which he creates his world: "I take it that God has made the world as it should be and that we can hardly hope to scrawl or daub anything better; our only aspiration should be to recreate modestly in His manner." And, like God, the artist has the ability to breathe life into inert matter; indeed, the artist's central function lies in his life-giving powers: "In all things I demand—life, the possibility of existence, and that's all; nor is it our business to ask whether it's beautiful, whether it's ugly. The feeling that there's life in the thing created is much more important than considerations of beauty and ugliness; it's the sole criterion in matters of art." To illustrate his theories,

Büchner's Lenz contrasts the two types of art—the one represented by the Apollo Belvedere and a Raphael Madonna, the other by two Dutch or Flemish genre paintings he had recently seen. He finds the former works too "idealized," and as a result "they make me feel quite dead." The genre paintings, which he goes on to describe in detail, "reproduce nature for me with the greatest degree of truthfulness, so that I can feel [the artist's] creation."

Except for a few remarks here and there in his letters, the discussion of aesthetics in *Lenz* is Büchner's only commentary on his own artistic ideals. But this discussion by no means provides a full rationale for his work; what it tells us—and quite appropriately so—is the points of contact he must have felt with the real Lenz. The analogy which it sets up between their literary art and genre paintings itself suggests the limits within which one may profitably compare their work. Lenz' best plays have something of the charm and the unpretentiousness which we associate with genre art, but they do not attempt to reach beyond the social frame of reference in which they are so securely rooted. (At the end of *The Private Tutor* and *The Soldiers* Lenz, in fact, shamelessly draws a pedantic social moral from his tale—a moral which, in each play, is quite inadequate to account for the richness of life which the play had seemed above all to depict.) Still, Lenz knew better than to attempt to ask the existential questions which echo so naturally out of Büchner's world. The range of reference encompassed by Büchner's plays is immeasurably wider than that of Lenz'. The discussion of aesthetics in Büchner's story, though it provides a rationale for his dramatic objectivity and his richness of detail, takes no account of many elements fundamental to his work—for example, the grotesque characterizations in *Woyzeck*, the verbal complexity and virtuosity of all three plays, the images of an inverted world which emerge out of *Danton's Death* and *Woyzeck*. Though Büchner's critics often depend on the discussion of aesthetics in *Lenz* to provide a theoretical framework for his art, one wonders if the statement, "I take it that God has made the world as it should be" (a statement, incidentally, which Büchner drew from Lenz' *Notes on the Theater*—1774), is really applicable to a body of work which continually voices its despair at the results of God's creation.

"The idealistic movement was just beginning at that time"—with these words, so fateful for Lenz, Büchner begins the discussion of aesthetics in his story. In 1778, the time in which the story takes place, Goethe was already firmly entrenched in the courtly world of Weimar and was working on *Iphigenia in Tauris*, the first of his major plays in his so-called "classical" manner. The Storm-and-Stress revolt had by this time spent its force (except for Schiller's explosive early plays, which date from the early '80's). For Lenz the advent of the "idealistic" period meant the end of a world in which he could feel himself significantly creative; the very basis of his talent was an earthy realism which the new art-ideals which were to emanate from Weimar for the next generation could scarcely accommodate.

By the time Büchner began to write, the "idealistic movement" (which German literary historians have conventionally divided into two phases—Classicism and Romanticism, the latter itself subdivided into two phases) had also spent its force. It was only natural for Büchner to seek a model in a writer from an earlier era. But Büchner's obvious antipathy to the plays which the idealistic movement produced must not blind us to the real and enduring achievement which marks this drama at its best. The major dramatic works of German Classicism, Goethe's *Iphigenia* (completed in 1786) and *Torquato Tasso* (1789) and Schiller's *Wallenstein* trilogy (1799), though they are little known today outside Germany, can easily hold their own among the world's great dramas. But a contemporary audience can scarcely approach them without some conception of the artistic and cultural premises on which they are based. For one thing, these plays are part of Goethe and Schiller's attempt to found a national culture, of which they saw a national drama as an indispensable cornerstone. Unlike England, France and Spain during their major periods of dramatic writing, Germany lacked a vital popular theatrical tradition; as a result, the plays of Goethe and Schiller often seem a kind of hothouse growth, nurtured with a deliberateness and high-mindedness which can all too easily create a barrier to modern taste.

The dramaturgy on which these plays is based is far more closely related to that of French seventeenth-century drama than it is to Shakespeare, though it is by no means a slavish imitation of earlier models, as was the earlier type of German drama represented by *The Dying Cato*. Compared to the Storm-and-Stress plays and Büchner's work, the German Classical plays remain essentially within the Aristotelian dramatic tradition. Their characters are invariably of high station. Their chief dramatic effects emerge out of a carefully contrived, though often relatively simple plot. In striking contrast to the Storm-and-Stress drama, they cultivate an economy of means, with the result that they sacrifice richness of detail for a more austere, lofty effect. Whereas the Storm-and-Stress plays, like Büchner's, were generally in prose, most of the Classical dramas are in blank verse—a verse, indeed, of a rather formal sort, with a diction and syntax deliberately removed from those of ordinary conversation. A work such as *Wallenstein* (which, though publicized and translated into English verse by so powerful a voice as Coleridge's, is scarcely known today to English-speaking readers) succeeds in creating a type of effect quite foreign to that of the various German anti-Aristotelian dramas before and after it. For in *Wallenstein* Schiller, like the ancient Greek tragedians, is centrally concerned with the mysteries inherent in a man's relation to his destiny; his dramatic method, with its cunning contrivance of plot, its disdain for "extraneous" detail, and its careful balance of concrete situation and abstract idea, allows the larger metaphysical questions to emerge naturally out of his fable with an intensity and singularity of effect which dramatists such as Büchner and Brecht have chosen to do without.

A sympathetic reading of the major German plays in

the "classical" manner suggests that the distinction which Büchner's Lenz draws between "idealized" and "real" characters is not altogether fair to the actual practice of Goethe and Schiller. The characters of *Wallenstein,* for instance, are "idealized" only to the extent that they speak a somewhat heightened language and are not depicted in the informal situations in which Büchner customarily presents his characters. But Schiller's characters at their best are also concretely differentiated from one another and, once one accepts the premises of his dramatic method, the reader or audience quite naturally comes to believe in them as living beings. Büchner, like any artist confronting a mode of art antithetical to his own, probably did not bother to distinguish between Schiller at his best and at his worst: his two recorded comments on Schiller, both of them negative, attack him for being too "rhetorical" and for creating characters who are essentially "puppets with sky-blue noses and affected pathos, but not flesh-and-blood human beings." [3] And with the notable exception of *Wallenstein* (and perhaps also his uncompleted play *Demetrius*—1805), one must admit that Büchner's view of Schiller's "classical" plays is more or less a just one. In a play such as *The Bride of Messina* (1802), a much more conscious attempt than *Wallenstein* to re-create the effect of Greek tragedy, Schiller's high-mindedness comes to seem virtually unbearable. And, quite in contrast to *Wallenstein,* such later historical plays as *The Maid of Orleans* (1801), *Mary Stuart* (1800) and *William Tell* (1804) fail to embody their lofty central "idea" in any concrete dramatic situation in which a modern audience can honestly believe.

By the time Büchner wrote his first play Schiller had been dead for thirty years and was firmly entrenched as the chief classic of the German theater. Indeed, the rhetoric and the "affected pathos" of which Büchner complains had become standard conventions of German drama—conventions so deeply rooted that the major German dramatists of our century have felt a continuing need to challenge them. It seems only natural that writers like

Gerhart Hauptmann and Brecht would look back to Büchner—as the latter looked back to Lenz—as a forerunner in their revolt against the Classical tradition in German drama.

But Büchner was not the first writer in his own century to challenge this tradition. At least two writers, Heinrich von Kleist and Christian Dietrich Grabbe, experimented with significantly new ways of dramatic expression. On the surface, at least, Kleist's plays seem to continue the Classical framework, for they utilize the basic conventions which Goethe and Schiller had established in their Classical plays. Kleist's major plays, *The Broken Jug* (1806), *Penthesilea* (1808), and *The Prince of Homburg* (1810), all maintain the formality of blank verse, and all are marked by the most rigorous economy of structure. Like the Classical plays before them, they are built out of a closely connected chain of events which lead up to the climax (the first two of these plays, though they are full length, each consist of a single, sustained act); and quite unlike Büchner's dramas they allow their central conflicts to develop through the direct confrontation of characters with one another.

Yet, despite his apparently traditional form, Kleist was far less an imitator than an innovator. His language, though elevated in diction, has a taut and breathless quality which, more than any other dramatic blank verse in German, creates the illusion of being spoken by living beings. Moreover, despite his Classical dramaturgy, which is predicated on the assumption that characters can express their conflicts with one another in verbal terms, his plays, like Büchner's, ultimately suggest the inability of human beings to communicate meaningfully at all. In *Penthesilea*, for example, the two chief characters appear to communicate with one another in an idyllic love scene, but the heroine, discovering that their relationship is based on a fundamental misunderstanding, ends up tricking her lover into a brutal death-trap. Kleist, one might say, exploits a dramatic method based on character relationships only to lay bare the deceptiveness inherent in these relationships. Like Büchner, Kleist was little known or appreciated in his own time; there is, in fact, no reason to think that Büchner discerned his real significance, if he read him at all. Yet despite their basic differences in dramatic technique, Kleist and Büchner share a certain kinship through the skepticism and the despair which their works voice with a notable lack of pretentiousness; and it hardly seems accidental that Kleist's plays, like Büchner's, achieved no general acclaim until our own century.

Grabbe, too, was little understood in his age. Although the quality of his achievement is considerably below that of Kleist and Büchner, his experiments in dramatic form anticipate much that Büchner was to develop in his own way. Grabbe's early plays are still largely in the grand style, and their blank verse betrays the staleness into which the language of Classical drama had fallen in the generation after Schiller. His heroes, quite in contrast to Büchner's, are also conceived in the grand manner; all, in fact, are men of titanic proportions—Napoleon, Hannibal, the Hohenstaufen emperors—who go to their doom through no fault of their own, but through the pettiness of a world which cannot support such titans. But Grabbe's later plays, above all *Napoleon or the Hundred Days* (1831) and *Hannibal* (1835), seem just as boldly "experimental" as *Danton's Death*.

Napoleon, which Büchner doubtless knew when he wrote his first play, presents a vast panoramic view of the events immediately leading up to Waterloo. Grabbe makes no attempt, as would a dramatist in the Classical tradition, to present these events in any causal chain. The play, in fact, is essentially a vivid and bounteous chronicle which focuses on such diverse phenomena as the crowds on the streets of Paris, soldiers in barracks on the eve of battle, the newly restored Bourbon court, and Napoleon vainly attempting to re-establish his past glory without realizing he lacked the means to do so. *Napoleon* is written in a terse and racy prose, a style which, unlike the verse of his earlier tragedies, is able to accommodate a wide variety of tones and to portray the historical milieu with a lively intimacy. In its mixture of comic and tragic elements, its technique of short, contrasting scenes, and its treatment of the common people caught up by vast historical forces, it may well have served as a model for *Danton's Death*. Though *Napoleon* still reads with a certain vitality, Grabbe did not, like Büchner, succeed in fusing the quite diverse components of his play to create a single, closely organized whole; and as a result, the play remains far more interesting in its individual details than in its totality. Above all, Grabbe lacks that quality of dramatic objectivity which I have tried to describe in Büchner's work. Karl Gutzkow tried to define this difference between the two writers in a letter he wrote to Büchner to encourage him in his work: "If one observes [Grabbe's] stiff, forced, bony manner, one must make the most favorable predictions for your fresh, effervescent natural powers." [4] If Gutzkow's statement is perhaps a bit unfair to Grabbe, it is also notable as the most powerful critical praise Büchner was to receive either in his lifetime or until half a century after his death.

ii

It is a tribute to the richness and variety of Büchner's achievement that each of the writers who have felt his impact have absorbed a different aspect of his work. Gerhart Hauptmann, the first major figure whom Büchner influenced, shares Büchner's sympathy for the sufferings of lowly people. Hauptmann's career, which spans almost six decades, includes a vast variety of forms and themes, from contemporary social realism to symbolic fantasy to grand-style tragedy based on Greek myth. But Hauptmann seems closest to Büchner in his early, largely realistic period. His short story, *The Apostle* (1890), a study of a modern religious fanatic, attempts to imitate the narrative method of Büchner's *Lenz;* yet Hauptmann's interior monologue today reads like a somewhat dated technical experiment, while Büchner's retains a freshness and naturalness which belie its great distance from us in time. Hauptmann perhaps came closest to the spirit of Büchner's work in his drama *The Weavers* (1892) which depicts an actual peasant uprising of the 1840's such as Büchner might have stirred up in his Giessen days. But Hauptmann's play is no socialist tract, as its early audiences often thought. Like Büchner in *Danton's Death*, Hauptmann questions the value of revolution while at the same time showing a high degree of sympathy for the grievances of the common people he is portraying.

In two later plays, *Henschel the Carter* (1898) and *Rose Bernd* (1903), Hauptmann, like Büchner in *Woyzeck*, succeeds in giving a traditional tragic dignity to inarticulate and passive characters of humble background. Hauptmann goes much further than Büchner in attempting to paint a detailed and authentic social milieu; indeed, the Silesian dialect of the original version of *The Weavers* would have proved so difficult for German readers that he had to "translate" the play into a more easily comprehensible form. Hauptmann's figures often have the brooding, explosive quality that he doubtless discerned in many of Büchner's figures, perhaps even in Büchner himself, whose genius Hauptmann once characterized as "glowing lava hurled out of Chthonic depths." [5] The characters and backgrounds of Hauptmann's best "realist" plays still seem impressive today, though his dramaturgy, with its well-wrought plots and his carefully planned motivations and foreshadowings, seems somewhat old-fashioned next to Büchner's, which shares the disdain for traditional theatrical effect of much contemporary drama.

If Hauptmann drew largely from the realistic side of Büchner's work, Frank Wedekind drew from the "unreal" side of Büchner, above all, the grotesque element which he discerned in the doctor, captain and carnival figures in *Woyzeck*. In his early play, *The Awakening of Spring* (1891), a violent and impassioned protest against the suppression of sexual knowledge in the education of the young, Wedekind depicts his middle-class characters as the kind of grotesque, perverted beings Büchner had presented before him. But Wedekind's entire poetic world is made up of grotesque types: the naturalness and dramatic objectivity with which characters such as Büchner's Marie, Marion and Danton are presented were totally foreign to Wedekind's talent. Ideologically, however, Wedekind's plays attempt to propagate a doctrine of naturalness; thus, in his character Lulu, the heroine of *The Earth Spirit* and its sequel, *Pandora's Box* (1895), Wedekind created a symbol of amoral and instinctual nature. As a literary type, Lulu is perhaps less akin to Büchner's Marie than to his drum major, whom she resembles in the exaggerated manner in which her "naturalness" is depicted.

Wedekind's success as a dramatic artist, one realizes today, falls short of his success as a liberating force in German culture at the turn of the century; though he was often capable of crudely powerful effects, he rarely succeeded in finding an adequate dramatic embodiment for the new ideas he was so intent on disseminating. Even if one admires his integrity, his Lulu, one must admit, is a rather dated creature who lives less surely in Wedekind's plays than in the opera which Alban Berg built around her. Through Wedekind, however, one side of Büchner—the rebel against bourgeois convention and the creator of the grotesquely extravagant language which Wedekind found in parts of *Woyzeck*—was transmitted to the Expressionist dramatists who followed him and, above all, to Bertolt Brecht.[6]

The fact that Berg's only two operas are based on *Woyzeck* and the Lulu plays is, I think, a testimony to the continuity which Berg's generation felt between Büchner's and Wedekind's work. Berg's setting (1921) of Büchner's play is itself an important instance of the impact of Büchner on our own century. Berg prepared his own libretto, and at first sight one feels amazed at how closely he followed Büchner's text. To be sure, he used only about two thirds of Büchner's scenes, and even these were sometimes pared down for economy's sake. But Berg stuck to the original dialogue to a relatively high degree and managed to retain much of the flavor of the play. His musical method, indeed, often succeeds in heightening Büchner's most original dramatic effects. For example, in Marie's repentance scene the music shifts back and forth in mood as Marie alternately reads from the Bible and expresses her own thoughts, and at the end of the scene it reaches a climax as piercing as any one might imagine from the text.

In its total effect, however, the opera seems a work of a very different kind from the play. Through the heavy orchestral commentary, which presents the composer's point of view on the events, the characters seem far less autonomous beings than they do in the original. The orchestra, in addition, serves to underline that sense of a malign fate which, because of the difference between the two media, hovers over the play in a far less distinct way. Indeed, the atonality of much of the music seems ideally suited to producing the eerie effects which Berg so obviously sought, especially in the final scenes. The character Wozzeck (whose name Berg spelled as it appeared in the Franzos edition of Büchner) seems even more passive and inarticulate than he does in the play. Among the passages which Berg cut out are those in which he asserts his dignity, for example the scene in which he gives Andres his belongings and reads his identification papers. Berg quite deliberately emphasized the abnormality and the suffering of his hero, who thus emerges as a helpless, crazed animal. Berg's version also stressed the economic degradation of the characters; in fact, the musical phrase which accompanies Wozzeck's words, "Wir arme Leut' "—"We poor folk"—is the chief leitmotif of the opera, achieving its fullest force in the long and powerful orchestral interlude which directly follows Wozzeck's suicide.

Berg's emphasis on the play's psychological and social aspects is accompanied by a lack of emphasis on the existential questions which Büchner poses so persistently throughout his work, for example in the complex man-animal imagery and in the grandmother's tale (of which Berg uses only a fragment). Büchner's existential questions depend, above all, on strictly literary means of expression for which Berg wisely did not seek a direct musical equivalent. Indeed, Büchner's basic dramatic method, with its loosely connected scenes which could seemingly be placed in several different combinations, in the opera becomes transformed into an entirely different mode of dramaturgy. Through the constant orchestral commentary, and, above all, through the interludes between scenes, each event seems to follow the last with the most frightening inevitability. Berg concentrates almost exclusively on the "main line" of plot and excludes everything that he must have thought subsidiary to it—for example, the carnival scenes, the conversation with the Jewish pawnbroker, in fact that whole crowded larger world which hovers around the edges of Büchner's play. Even the comic touches, grim as they are in the play, are almost missing from the opera; one is scarcely tempted to laugh during the scene between Wozzeck and the doctor, and largely, I think, because of the quite uncomic effect of the musical accompaniment (partly also because Berg, who was perhaps worried about getting his work performed, shifted the doctor's experiment from the excretory to the respiratory functions). The opera, as a result, has a kind of classical starkness and solemnity quite foreign to the spirit of the play. It seems to me symptomatic of Berg's classicism that every scene consists of a different musical form, each systematically different from the others. The following summary,[7] based on Berg's stated intentions, suggests the form-consciousness which governs the opera (scene numbers in parentheses, music in italics):

Act I. Exposition, Wozzeck and his relation to his environment / *five character sketches:* (1) the captain / *suite;* (2) Andres / *rhapsody;* (3) Marie / *military march and cradle song;* (4) the physician / *passacaglia;* (5) the drum major / *andante affettuoso* (*quasi rondo*).

Act II. Dénouement, Wozzeck is gradually convinced of Marie's infidelity / *symphony in five movements:* (1) Wozzeck's first suspicion / *sonata form;* (2) Wozzeck is mocked / *fantasie and fugue;* (3) Wozzeck accuses Marie / *largo;* (4) Marie and drum major dance / *scherzo;* (5) the drum major trounces Wozzeck / *rondo martiale.*

Act III. Catastrophe, Wozzeck murders Marie and atones through suicide/*six inventions:* (1) Marie's remorse / *invention on a theme;* (2) death of Marie / *invention on a tone;* (3) Wozzeck tries to forget / *invention on a rhythm;* (4) Wozzeck drowns in the pond / *invention on a six-tone chord; instrumental interlude* with closed curtain; (5) Marie's son plays unconcerned / *invention on a persistent rhythm* (*perpetuum mobile*).

Berg himself tells us that he chose such diverse forms to embody each scene in order to avoid the effect of musical monotony.[8] One must admit, surely, that even after repeated hearings the listener remains unaware of the nature of the various forms which Berg employs. Yet the form-consciousness which is manifest in the above chart is indicative, I think, of a kind of classicism peculiar to much of the art of the 1920's. It seems to me analogous, for instance, to the mythological framework and charts of correspondences around which James Joyce constructed *Ulysses;* T. S. Eliot's well-known description of the function of Joyce's mythological framework—"It is simply a way of controlling, of ordering, of giving a shape and a significance to the immense panorama of futility and anarchy which is contemporary history"[9]—is perhaps applicable to the function of the tight musical forms which Berg employs to contain the chaotic and characteristically modern materials that he found in Büchner's play. The resulting opera achieves a greatness that remains independent of that of the play; one recognizes it as a work of equal, though by no means kindred genius. Since Berg's work has made its way in recent years into the repertory of all the major opera houses, one hopes that the strong competition it offers will not exclude the play from theatrical performance, which, up to now, it has rarely achieved in the English-speaking countries.

Our sense of Büchner's modernity has been shaped to a large degree through his impact upon, and his affinities with the two most significant developments in European theater during the last few decades—the work of Bertolt Brecht, on the one hand, and the *avant garde* theater in

Paris after World War II. It was only natural that Brecht should look back to Büchner as an example: not only did Brecht view Büchner as a fellow political revolutionary, but Büchner's work stood for many of the same values that Brecht throughout his life sought to articulate. Both writers, for instance, succeeded in creating a vital and glowing dramatic language by first refusing to be poetic in any traditional way. Like Büchner, Brecht created an idiom of his own, colloquial, earthy, ironical—an idiom, moreover, which appears to imitate the language of real men, yet which in its total effect has a richly poetic resonance. Brecht's, like Büchner's, is a realism which refuses to be pedantically realistic: the red moon which hovers menacingly over the murder scene in *Woyzeck* was conceived in something of the same spirit as the red moon which, at the end of Brecht's early play *Drums in the Night* (1919), turns out to be a Chinese lantern which the embittered hero angrily destroys.

Brecht's language is perhaps most directly imitative of Büchner's in his first play, *Baal* (1918), whose bohemian hero speaks a wildly extravagant language which Brecht, like Wedekind before him, developed from such examples as Woyzeck's descriptions of his visions and such caricatures as Büchner's doctor, captain and carnival figures. But Brecht's affinities with Büchner cannot be defined simply through such instances of imitation; one could argue, in fact, that the personal idiom he achieved in his more mature work, through its poise and control, has more in common with Büchner's language than anything in *Baal*. Both writers, moreover, attain much of their creative impulse through their conscious opposition to the conventions of the German Classical drama. For Brecht, as for Wedekind, Büchner served as a kind of liberating force, not only against the Classical drama, but against the middle-class values with which this drama was associated in their minds. The Schiller-like rhetoric which Büchner parodies in the speeches of the drunken stage-prompter Simon in *Danton's Death* is sustained through two full-length plays by Brecht, *St. Joan of the Stockyards* (1930) and *The Resistible Rise of Arturo Ui* (1941), whose intentionally pompous blank verse succeeds in parodying not so much the Chicago capitalists who are made to speak it as the middle-class Germans whose slavish awe of their theatrical classics was for Brecht a sure symptom of their false cultural values.

Not only must Brecht have discerned in Büchner a fellow enemy of theatrical rhetoric, but the forms of organization which Büchner developed in his three plays provided the most successful German example before Brecht of a non-Aristotelian serious drama. In certain crucial respects—for instance, in their disdain for linear plots and their stress on the relative independence of individual scenes—Büchner's plays can surely be seen as ancestors of Brecht's "epic" theater. But Brecht's much-publicized theoretical pronouncements on the nature of epic theater cannot be applied literally to Büchner's plays, nor, it could be argued, to Brecht's own best works; the so-called "alienation effect," whereby the audience is discouraged from believing in the literal reality of the events enacted onstage, is scarcely applicable to plays such as *Danton's Death* and *Woyzeck*, whose dramatic reality we are made to accept wholeheartedly and with whose heroes we sympathize to a high degree. Although Brecht attempted to create most of his heroes as didactic negative examples and to hold back the audience's sympathy with them, some of his greatest figures—for instance, the cowardly Galileo, the greedy vendor Mother Courage, the alternately hearty and sour Finnish businessman Mr. Puntila—despite their author's intentions, achieve something of the autonomous life and the sympathetic quality which we find in Büchner's Danton and Woyzeck.

Like Büchner, Brecht has a penchant for passive heroes who allow the world to shape them as it will; Brecht, indeed, has perhaps gone further than any major dramatist in exploring the psychology of passivity—for instance, in the well-meaning porter Galy Gay in *Man Equals Man* (1926), who is cajoled into assuming the identity of another man and becoming a brutal soldier; in the hero of

The Life of Galileo (1939), who compromises his principles for the sake of bodily comfort and privacy to pursue his writings; in the good soldier Schweik, who, transferred by Brecht from Jaroslav Hašek's novel (itself an extension of the comic possibilities in the character of Woyzeck) to a more modern setting in *Schweik in the Second World War* (1944), manages to survive and sometimes even to confound the Nazis by pretending to comply with them.

The essential humanitarianism which underlies both Büchner's and Brecht's work finds expression partly through their common skepticism toward older forms of humanitarianism which they see as false or stale. The skepticism with which Büchner treats the doctor's traditionally idealistic definitions of the human being finds its modern equivalent in such Brechtian formulations as the title and theme of *Man Equals Man*, which attempts to demonstrate that one human being *can* be changed into another, or Macheath's cynical refrain in *The Threepenny Opera* (1928):

> *What does a man live by? By grinding, sweating,*
> *Defeating, beating, cheating, eating some other man*
> *For he can only live by sheer forgetting*
> *Forgetting that he ever was a man.*[10]

The title of the parable play *The Good Person* [*Der gute Mensch*] *of Setzuan* (1940) seems almost an echo of the phrase which Büchner ironically puts into the captain's mouth time and again—"Woyzeck, du bist ein guter Mensch, ein guter Mensch"; the captain's phrase is as empty of real meaning as is the title of Brecht's play, whose parable attempts to demonstrate the impossibility of being "good" in the world as it is. Just as the work of both writers achieved a poetic quality only after their deliberate rejection of older, staler forms of poetic language, so it succeeds in expounding a humanitarianism through their tough-minded distrust of smug, traditional ethical statements.

It seems no accident that Büchner achieved his first major acclaim outside Germany in the French theater of the last two decades, for his plays anticipate many of the themes and techniques of the so-called "theater of the absurd." One might note, for instance, the following passage from the promenade scene in *Danton's Death* (Act II, Scene 2), in which Büchner records the conversation of two gentlemen walking along the street:

FIRST GENTLEMAN You know, it is the most extraordinary discovery! I mean, it makes all the branches of science look entirely different. Mankind really is striding towards its high destiny.

SECOND GENTLEMAN Have you seen that new play? There's a great Babylonian tower, a mass of arches and steps and passages, and then, do you know, they blow the whole thing up, right into the air, just like that! It makes you dizzy. Quite extraordinary. [*He stops, perplexed.*]

FIRST GENTLEMAN Why, whatever's the matter?

SECOND GENTLEMAN Oh, nothing, really! But—would you just give me a hand—over this puddle—there! Thank you very much. I only just got over it. That could be extremely dangerous!

FIRST GENTLEMAN You weren't afraid of it, were you?

SECOND GENTLEMAN Well, yes—the earth's only a very thin crust, you know. I always think I might fall through where there's a hole like that. You have to walk very gently or you may easily go through. But do go and see that play—I thoroughly recommend it!

This passage could easily be mistaken for one of the random street conversations which one finds, say, in *The Killer* (1957) by Eugène Ionesco, who himself once listed Büchner, in company with Aeschylus, Sophocles, Shakespeare, and Kleist, as the only dramatist of the past whom he still found readable.[11]

Büchner, like Ionesco in similar passages, provides no context for this conversation: we are never told, for instance, what sort of scientific discovery the first gentleman is even talking about; much of the comic effect, indeed, comes from Büchner's deliberate failure to provide any context at all for the gentleman's pretentious remarks.

Like the recent French dramatists, Büchner is concerned with exposing the emptiness inherent in the clichés with which people customarily express themselves ("Mankind . . . striding towards its high destiny"). By attempting to record conversation as it is really spoken—not, as in earlier drama, as it *ought* to be spoken—he exposes, as well, the absurdity of the transitions within ordinary human speech: the second gentleman, for example, moves unself-consciously from his enthusiasm for a new play to his fear of the hole in the street and then, at the end of the passage (which is also the end of the scene) directly back to the play in question. If one examines the transition (or lack of it) from the first to the second speech, one notes that the characters are shown talking *past* one another instead of *with* one another. Indeed, there is no real contact between them: the first is fully concerned with his statement about some scientific discovery, the second with his enthusiasm for a play he has seen. In thus demonstrating that human beings often fail to make contact even while they appear to be conversing, Büchner anticipates a technique that was not to be exploited to any great degree in drama until Chekhov and the recent French dramatists. The difficulty of human communication is not merely the theme of this small passage, but is, after all, one of the central themes of *Danton's Death* as a whole: one need only remember Danton's statement to his wife, on the first page of the play, of the impossibility of people really knowing one another. And it is a central theme, moreover, in such otherwise diverse contemporary plays as Arthur Adamov's *The Parody* (1947), Ionesco's *The Bald Soprano* (1948), and Beckett's *Waiting for Godot* (1952).

In fact, to catalogue the themes of the "theater of the absurd" is at once to catalogue many of Büchner's essential themes. The terror, absurd and frightening at once, which lurks behind Adamov's *The Large and the Small Maneuver* (1950) and *Each against Each* (1952) is similar in kind to the terror in the background of *Danton's Death*, which Adamov had himself translated into French a few years before completing these plays; moreover, the totalitarian political rhetoric which resounds in both plays is essentially a modern version of the brutally lifeless language of Robespierre's and St. Just's public pronouncements. The skepticism towards their self-identity which plagues the central characters of *Waiting for Godot* and Adamov's *Professor Taranne* (1951) has much in common with Leonce's skepticism in Büchner's comedy. The vaudeville routines which Beckett's clowns use to while away the time that hangs so oppressively on them corresponds quite precisely to the *commedia dell'arte* techniques employed by Leonce and Valerio to fulfill the same purpose.[12] Indeed, the very words with which Didi in *Waiting for Godot* voices his boredom and despair might easily have come from one of Danton's, or Leonce's, or Lenz' speeches: "We wait. We are bored. No, don't protest, we are bored to death, there's no denying it. Good. A diversion comes along and what do we do? We let it go to waste. Come, let's get to work! In an instant all will vanish and we'll be alone once more, in the midst of nothingness!" [13]

In the face of such an insight, voiced with equal emphasis by Büchner and Beckett, all human endeavor comes to seem futile, meaningless, and absurd. As Lee Baxandall has suggested in his essay on *Danton's Death*, the agonized lyricism of Büchner's first play "finds its closest modern counterpart" in *Waiting for Godot*.[14] And it is through this lyricism, one might add, that Beckett, more than any of his contemporaries, has captured that sense of mystery which ultimately stands behind the despair in Büchner's plays. Moreover, through its plotlessness, its vagueness of setting, and its lack of any real social framework, *Waiting for Godot* seems a kind of Büchner play with its narrative and its background removed. Or, rather, one could view it as a more radical step than the ones Büchner had taken in *Danton's Death* and *Woyzeck* to break down the canons of classical drama.

Yet a comparison of Büchner with the recent French dramatists also suggests some vital differences in purpose and form between his work and theirs. However strikingly

Büchner's work may anticipate the significant experiments of our time, it also, for instance, employs certain traditional methods of characterization which the French dramatists have largely abandoned. Thus, Büchner attempted, as the French have chosen not to, to create the illusion of a full and varied world of real beings rooted in a real and recognizable environment. Marie in *Woyzeck* has a completeness and a reality that go well beyond her dramatic function in the play; when she sits before the mirror admiring her new earrings she gains our sympathy in a way that no character—except, perhaps, some of Beckett's—in any of the recent French plays can. Directly after the execution of the Dantonists, a woman passerby makes the sort of statement one often finds in Ionesco's plays: "I always say you ought to see a man in different surroundings; I'm all for these public executions, aren't you, love?" But the effect of these lines is shattering in a way that they could not be in Ionesco. Because of the interest and sympathy which Danton and his friends have aroused in us throughout the play, the passerby's statement causes us to feel at once the tragedy and the absurdity of their death. In contrast, the ironic statements made by the maid in Ionesco's *The Lesson* (1950) after the professor, in a fit of ire, has stabbed his pupil, suggest only the absurdity of the pupil's death. Ionesco, one might say, has dehumanized his characters in order to portray the precariousness and isolation in which they exist, while Büchner has demonstrated a similar precariousness and isolation by more traditional means—by first making us believe in the reality of his characters and their background. In the world of Büchner's plays we still feel the plenitude of creation, even if God's traditional beneficence is missing and his existence is, at most, a questionable thing.

iii

The vitality and the fullness of vision which characterize Büchner's dramatic world have rarely been achieved by those whom he has influenced, perhaps only by Brecht, but these qualities are present in far greater abundance in the dramatist whose impact Büchner felt more strongly than that of any other, namely, Shakespeare. Shakespeare, indeed, is the one writer for whom Büchner expressed the highest and most unqualified admiration. "Poor Shakespeare was a clerk by day and had to write his poetry at night, and I, who am not worthy to untie his shoelaces, have a much easier time," Büchner wrote to his fiancée a few weeks before his death.[15] In his first letter to Gutzkow, when excusing himself for not being entirely true to history in *Danton's Death*, he consoled himself with the notion that "all poets, with the exception of Shakespeare, confront history and nature as though they were school-boys." [16] The "fullness of life" which Büchner's character Lenz upholds so passionately as the central goal of art can be found only—thus we are told in the story—in Shakespeare and in folk poetry, and sometimes in Goethe—"everything else should be thrown in the fire." Like nearly all German writers for at least a generation before him, Büchner had been smitten by Shakespeare's plays since childhood; one of his Darmstadt schoolmates, in fact, testifies how Büchner and his friends would go to a nearby beech forest to read Shakespeare to one another on Sunday afternoons.[17]

The many verbal echoes from Shakespeare in Büchner's work have been scrupulously recorded by various scholars,[18] and I shall not attempt to add to their findings here. It seems no surprise to find that Büchner echoed *Hamlet* more than any other Shakespearean play, indeed more than any other literary work. The influence of *Hamlet* went considerably beyond the verbal level. In their passivity, their introspectiveness and their verbal ingenuity, characters like Danton and Leonce obviously have something of Hamlet in them, though they derive as much from the various Hamlet-like heroes of German Romanticism as from the character actually created by Shakespeare. In her pathos and madness Lucille, in *Danton's Death*, has certain affinities with Ophelia. The deathly atmosphere, moreover, which permeates Büchner's first play has much in common with the atmosphere of Shakespeare's play.

It is worth noting, furthermore, that Büchner sometimes

resorted to Shakespeare during the tensest dramatic moments of his plays. When Lucille laments the death of her husband, she speaks like Lear on the death of Cordelia: "Dying–dying–! But everything lives, everything's got to live, I mean, the little fly there, the bird. Why can't he?" Woyzeck's last words, in turn, echo Lady Macbeth's feelings of guilt: "Am I still bloody? I better wash up. There's a spot and there's another." Only a dramatist in another language would dare echo such familiar lines at such crucial moments in his own work; for an English dramatist to do so would be to risk writing a parody.

More significant than such echoes is the fact that Büchner succeeded–better, perhaps, than any other German dramatist–in imitating Shakespeare's manner while at the same time integrating it fully into the contexts he himself was creating. His Shakespearean imitation is most fully evident in *Danton's Death*, and it becomes progressively less evident in each of his two other plays. The following passage, in which the carters standing outside the Conciergerie are waiting to take Danton and his friends to the guillotine, has a genuinely Shakespearean quality about it (more so, I might add, in the German than in translation):

SECOND CARTER Well, who would you say was the best carters?

FIRST CARTER Whoever goes farthest and quickest.

SECOND CARTER Well, you old fool, you can't cart a man much further than out of this world, can you, and I'd like to see anyone do it in less than a quarter of an hour. It's exactly a quarter of an hour from here to Guillotine Square.

JAILER Hurry up, you lazy slugs! Get in nearer the gate. Get back a bit, you girls.

FIRST CARTER No, don't you budge! Never go round a girl, always go through.

SECOND CARTER I'm with you there. You can take your horse and cart in with you, the roads are nice, but you'll be in quarantine when you come out again. [*They move forward*.] What are you gawping at?

A WOMAN Waiting to see our old customers, dearie.

SECOND CARTER My cart's not a brothel, you know. This is a decent cart, this is; the King went in this, and all the big nobs in Paris.

The bawdy and far-fetched jokes are obviously typical of the banter of Shakespeare's clowns and fools. But Büchner has not only captured the tone of this banter, he has also understood the dramatic function which this sort of banter has in a Shakespearean tragedy. Like the gravedigger scene in *Hamlet,* this passage creates a needed slackening of tension between the two anguished scenes in the Conciergerie immediately before and after it. Yet, also like the gravedigger scene, it functions as something more than "comic relief." Although we laugh at the jokes, the dramatic context in which they are placed powerfully qualifies the effect they have on us. There is something rather grotesque, after all, in the carter's concern for his social status ("this is a decent cart, this is; the King went in this") in the inverted world of the Reign of Terror: indeed, there is something even frightening about it, since he is about to cart the play's hero to his death. The fusion of comic and tragic which we see here and elsewhere in Büchner is a peculiarly Shakespearean one—a fusion, moreover, which is effected not only through the alternation of comic and tragic scenes, but through the multiplicity of levels (ironic, grotesque, pathetic, or whatever) with which a single speech, a single image even, may be interpreted. One could argue, in fact, that Büchner seems modern to us in many of the same respects in which he seems most Shakespearean. Through his use of comic techniques to express the most desperate human situations, his plays as surely look backward to Shakespeare—for instance, to Lear's scenes with his fool—as they look forward to the clowning in *Waiting for Godot.*

Büchner's Shakespearean quality is discernible not only through his echoes and his conscious attempts at imitation, but in certain fundamental affinities he shares with Shakespeare. Büchner is Shakespearean, for instance, in the dramatic objectivity with which most of his characters are conceived and in the consequent impersonality he achieves in relation to his work. His talent is akin to that which Keats, in a famous passage from one of his letters, was trying to define when he distinguished his own and Shakespeare's mode from that of Wordsworth: "A Poet [by which Keats here means one like Shakespeare or himself] is the most unpoetical of any thing in existence; because he has no Identity—he is continually . . . filling some other Body—The Sun, the Moon, the Sea and Men and Women who are creatures of impulse are poetical and have about them an unchangeable attribute—the poet has none." [19] Like Shakespeare, Büchner expunges his own identity in favor of that of his characters, who seem to live with an autonomous and spontaneous life of their own. Of the major German dramatists before Büchner, only Goethe, I think, possessed this quality, though the severely classicist directions which Goethe's work, including his methods of characterization, took after his Storm-and-Stress years gave it an increasingly less Shakespearean character.

Büchner's most fundamental Shakespearean quality lies, perhaps, in his conception of a drama as a fully embodied poetic world of its own, relying as much on its richness of verbal texture as on its narrative to achieve its effects. The image of a crazy upside-down world which Büchner achieved in *Woyzeck* is comparable in kind, if not in degree, to the image out of which a play such as *King Lear* is built. The power that emanates from both these works is due as much to the atmosphere created by such indirect means as images and ironic thematic parallels as it is to the simple facts of "plot"; both plays, in fact, create their image of a distorted world partly, at least, through their constant insistence on the animallike nature of men—*Lear*, for instance, through its persistent imagery of wild animals, *Woyzeck* through such passages as the animal demonstrations in the carnival scenes. The non-Aristotelian conception of drama in which Büchner seems so conspicuously a pioneer is in certain respects, at least, a Shakespearean conception, as it was, indeed, for the German Storm-and-Stress writers, with whom Büchner felt such obvious affinities. Modern Shakespeare critics such as G. Wilson Knight and William Empson no longer read Shakespeare in terms of the expositions and dénouements with which their classicist-minded predecessors were all too often concerned, but attempt instead to describe and explore the larger poetic whole which they see in each play.[20] Büchner, I think, discerned Shakespeare's dramatic method in something of the way we see it today, and to the extent that his plays achieve a Shakespearean thickness of texture and concentration of meaning, he seems to me the most Shakespearean of German dramatists.

iv

Even though Büchner's most striking affinities are with dramatists who lived long before or after him, in certain limited respects he is peculiarly of his own time. His work seems little related, however, to the German drama of the period; except for Grabbe, whose possible influence I noted earlier, the significant dramatic writing of the 1830's took directions quite different from Büchner's. The work of the Viennese comic writers Ferdinand Raimund and Johann Nestroy derives directly from the popular theater of Vienna, the only German-speaking city which had maintained a living *commedia dell'arte* tradition. Franz Grillparzer, also a Viennese, succeeded in giving new life to the forms of the German Classical drama, which he was able to fuse with elements derived from Spanish drama and the Viennese folk tradition. If there was any contemporary dramatist for whom Büchner could feel any real affinities, it was one who did not write in German at all, namely Musset, from whom, as I indicated in my chapter on *Leonce and Lena,* he borrowed what he found useful, and no more.

Nor can one discern many significant relationships between Büchner and the German nondramatic writers of his time. When Büchner was mentioned by nineteenth- and early twentieth-century literary historians his name was usually lumped together with those of the Young

Germany group, men such as Gutzkow, Heinrich Laube, and Ludwig Wienbarg—and for no better reason than that he was politically on the left and had been sponsored by Gutzkow. Even without Büchner's firm denial of sympathy with the aims and ideas of the Young Germans,[21] one need only set their works next to his to note a fundamental difference both in their essential thematic concerns and their artistic stature. Gutzkow's best-known work, his short novel *Wally the Doubter,* written in the same year (1835) in which Büchner began his correspondence with him, attempts, far more than any of Büchner's works, to deal with a characteristic contemporary problem, the "problem of the modern woman"; when we read it today, however, *Wally* seems less about any real woman than about a problem which Gutzkow lacked the means to embody in any artistically convincing way.

Of the most notable German poets writing in the 1830's—namely, Heinrich Heine, Annette von Droste-Hülshoff, and Eduard Mörike—only Heine shares something of Büchner's world. Büchner himself probably never appreciated Heine's real distinction, for he listed his name with those of the Young Germans (to whom Heine can be linked only superficially) whom he rejected.[22] The common spirit of the age which shapes the work of both manifests itself in their ironical perspectives and their ability to endow seemingly trivial and prosaic situations with poetic meaning; yet the sensibility that emerges from the writings of each—Heine's work is built around his personality, whereas Büchner's is notable for the deliberate absence of the author's personality—is as different as that of any two writers can be.[23]

The spirit of Büchner's age cannot be defined merely by the organized movements of the time—Young Germany, for instance, or Romanticism in France and Italy—but by the work of certain lonely figures who, in one way or another, were at war with their time. Büchner's closest contemporaries were perhaps less his fellow writers in German than such figures as Stendhal and Lermontov. Each of these, though rooted in the Romantic Movement within his particular country, is distinguished by the concretely real world he created in his fiction and by the steadfast ironic control he maintained over his material.

The major novels of Stendhal, who was thirty years older than Büchner, were written during the same decade which witnessed Büchner's brief career; Lermontov, who was a year younger than Büchner and died only four years after him, reached his artistic maturity in the last years of the decade. Both writers, like Büchner, have succeeded in making contact with our own century with an immediacy which few other nineteenth-century writers were able to achieve. Büchner was further removed from Romanticism (which had waned in Germany far earlier than in France or Russia) than were the authors of *Racine and Shakespeare* or the Byronic narratives that marked Lermontov's early period.[24] Yet it could be argued that each of these writers seems most modern to us in precisely those areas in which he found the means to distance himself from the various Romantic themes and conventions which he inherited. Pechorin, the protagonist of Lermontov's *A Hero of Our Time* (1840), speaks more directly to us than any of Byron's heroes (including even Don Juan) because Lermontov has created a recognizable social environment for him and, above all, has been willing to view him ironically from a number of points of view. We are willing to accept Julien Sorel, in *The Red and the Black* (1830), as a hero only because Stendhal has placed his heroic gestures in an environment in which they come to seem useless and absurd. At one point in this novel (Book II, Chapter XII) Mathilde looks back longingly to the heroic days of the Revolution and imagines her lover Julien in the role of Danton. Büchner, one might say, went one step further than Stendhal: the banality which Stendhal attributed to the world of the Restoration is much the same as the banality which Büchner discerned in the Revolution as well. The imaginary commonwealth which Stendhal depicted in *The Charterhouse of Parma* (1838) is much akin—above all, in its attempt to hold on to long-outmoded institutions—to the grand duchy of Hesse in which Büchner grew up. If Büchner had lived on to write a drama or novel on Hesse, the image that might have emerged would, I think, have had more in common with Stendhal's ironic portrait of Parma than with the more simple-minded revolutionist's image of Hesse which Büchner presented in *The Hessian Messenger*.

In Stendhal, Lermontov, and Büchner the modern reader recognizes a complexity of intelligence and a dramatic objectivity relatively rare in the work of their Romantic contemporaries and predecessors, whose virtues are of a different, less characteristically modern kind. The realism of these three writers is less amply detailed than that of Balzac or such later writers as Flaubert and Zola; yet it is a realism as surely rooted in their contemporary worlds as that of any writer who came after them. The ironical perspectives which govern the work of all three are centrally directed to laying bare pretensions and uncovering the shades of meaning that lie beneath pat assertions and dramatic postures. Büchner's skepticism, more than that of Stendhal or Lermontov, is a skepticism without poses; the dramatic form he employed (as well as the type of fiction with which he experimented in *Lenz*) gave him little opportunity to put on masks of his own. His manner is perhaps less urbane than that of Stendhal or Lermontov; yet his irony is reinforced more powerfully than theirs by memorable images of terror and suffering. Whatever labels we ultimately attach to such writers—post-Romantic, say, or proto-Modern—their work leads us to question the conventional time divisions with which we have learned to look at literary history.

NOTES

1—*The Biographical Background*

1. Büchner, *Werke und Briefe,* ed. Fritz Bergemann (Wiesbaden, 1958), p. 406. This edition will henceforth be cited as "Bergemann." I have drawn the biographical information for this chapter from a number of sources, the most important being Bergemann's edition, which includes letters by and to Büchner plus a number of reminiscences by his friends. For his career as revolutionist I have used Karl Viëtor's *Georg Büchner als Politiker* (Berne, 1939) and *Georg Büchner: Politik, Dichtung, Wissenschaft* (Berne, 1949); the discussion of his scientific career is based on the latter book and Jean Strohl's *Lorenz Oken und Georg Büchner* (Zurich, 1936).

2. Bergemann, p. 447.

3. *Ibid.*, p. 368.

4. *Ibid.*, p. 373.

5. *Ibid.*, pp. 374–75, 379–80.

6. *Ibid.*, p. 376.

7. *Ibid.*, p. 391.

8. *Ibid.*, p. 465.

9. *Ibid.*, p. 586.

10. *Ibid.*, p. 422.

11. *Ibid.*, p. 580. The religious implications of this statement for *Woyzeck* are taken up, for instance, by Benno von Wiese in *Die deutsche Tragödie von Lessing bis Hebbel* (Hamburg, 1948), II, 325–33, and by Franz Mautner in "Wortgewebe, Sinngefüge und 'Idee' in Büchners 'Woyzeck,'" *Deutsche Vierteljahrsschrift,* XXXV (1961), 543–47.

12. Bergemann, in his edition, passionately defends Minna Jaeglé against the charges that past scholars have made against her (pp. 616–17).

13. *Ibid.*, pp. 597–98.

14. For a comprehensive history of Büchner on the German stage, see Ingeborg Strudthoff, *Die Rezeption Georg Büchners durch das deutsche Theater* (Berlin, 1957).

2—*Danton's Death: Antirhetoric and Dramatic Form*

1. I refer to Joseph Frank's well-known discussion of the fair scene in *Madame Bovary* in his essay "Spatial Form in Modern Literature," *Sewanee Review*, LIII (1945), 230–2. The "counterpoint" of this scene was a new technique in fiction, though it was a quite traditional technique in drama, at least in farce or in serious drama outside the classical tradition.

2. Helmut Krapp, *Der Dialog bei Georg Büchner* (Darmstadt, 1958), pp. 15–19.

3. In his critical edition of *Danton's Death* Richard Thieberger provides a useful collation of sources and text. See *La Mort de Danton et ses sources* (Paris, 1953), pp. 35–52.

4. "Some Büchner Letters in Translation," trans. K. W. Maurer, *German Life and Letters*, VIII (1954), 52.

5. Wolfgang Martens, in his article "Zum Menschenbild Georg Büchners: 'Woyzeck' und die Marionszene in 'Dantons Tod,'" *Wirkendes Wort*, VIII (1957), 13–20, carefully defines Marion's uniqueness as a literary figure and links her to Büchner's thematic preoccupations in *Woyzeck*.

6. See, for instance, Karl Viëtor's discussion of the relationship of the two characters in *Georg Büchner: Politik, Dichtung, Wissenschaft*, pp. 107–8.

7. One might note that the historical Thomas Paine professed a deistic creed and not the atheism which Büchner's character defends. See Rudolf Majut, "Georg Büchner and Some English Thinkers," *Modern Language Review*, XLVIII (1953), 313–14.

8. *Samuel Beckett: The Language of Self* (Carbondale, Ill., 1962), p. 59.

9. *Georg Büchner: Politik, Dichtung, Wissenschaft*, p. 152.

10. "Georg Büchner's *Danton's Death*," *Tulane Drama Review*, VI (1962), 148.

11. "Some Büchner Letters," trans. Maurer, p. 52.

12. Heinrich von Treitschke, *Deutsche Geschichte im neunzehnten Jahrhundert* (Leipzig, 1907), IV, 434.

13. See Ralph P. Rosenberg, "Georg Büchner's Early Reception in America," *Journal of English and Germanic Philology*, XLIV (1945), 270–73.

14. See Strudthoff, pp. 52–55.

15. "Der faschistisch verfälschte und der wirkliche Georg Büchner," in *Deutsche Realisten des neunzehnten Jahrhunderts* (Berlin, 1952), pp. 75–78. For a more sensitive Marxist interpretation of the play, see Hans Mayer, *Georg Büchner und seine Zeit* (Berlin, 1960), pp. 182–207.

16. The most extreme nihilist interpretation is that of Robert Mühlher, "Georg Büchner und die Mythologie des Nihilismus," in *Dichtung der Krise* (Vienna, 1951), pp. 97–146. Benno von Wiese's interpretation in *Die deutsche Tragödie von Lessing bis Hebbel*, II, 309–33, also stresses the nihilistic element, but far more moderately and responsibly than Mühlher does.

17. For instance, Walter Höllerer, in his chapter on *Danton's Death* contributed to *Das deutsche Drama*, ed. Benno von Wiese (Düsseldorf, 1962), II, 65–88; Gerhart Baumann, *Georg Büchner: Die dramatische Ausdruckswelt* (Göttingen, 1961), pp. 9–87; and Wolfgang Martens, "Ideologie und Verzweiflung: Religiöse Motive in Büchners Revolutionsdrama," *Euphorion*, LIV (1960), 83–108.

18. *Politics and the Novel* (New York, 1957), p. 22.

19. Bergemann, p. 350.

20. "Some Letters," trans. Maurer, p. 51.

21. See, for instance, two of his letters to Gutzkow, in Bergemann, pp. 396, 412.

22. *Ibid.*, p. 339.

23. "From Georg Büchner's Letters," trans. Maurice Edwards, *Tulane Drama Review*, VI (1962), 134–35.

24. Bergemann, pp. 377–78.

25. See, for instance, Rudolf Majut's detailed study of the literary traditions—both before and after Büchner—to which characters such as Danton and Leonce belong. *Studien um Büchner: Untersuchungen zur Geschichte der problematischen Natur* (Berlin, 1932).

26. It is worth noting that Büchner chose to omit an important detail which his sources suggested at this point—

Lacroix's reproach that Danton's failure to heed the warnings he had received was responsible for the arrest of his friends: "You knew it," cried Lacroix, "and you failed to act! Now see the result of your habitual sloth; it has caused our downfall" (quoted by Thieberger, p. 45). Büchner's inclusion of this reproach would have undercut the audience's sense of the unquestioningly loyal attitude which Danton's friends seem to have toward him.

27. "Tod und Witz im Werke Georg Büchners," *Monatshefte für den deutschen Unterricht*, XLVI (1954), 123–36.

28. "Some Letters," trans. Maurer, p. 50.

29. Thieberger, p. 52.

3—*Leonce and Lena: Comedy as a Diversion from Despair*

1. Viëtor, *Georg Büchner: Politik, Dichtung, Wissenschaft*, p. 179.

2. For a comprehensive list of Büchner's borrowings from Musset, see Maurice Gravier, "Georg Büchner et Alfred de Musset," *Orbis Litterarum*, IX (1954), 29–44, and Henri Plard, "A propos de *Leonce und Lena:* Musset et Büchner," *Etudes germaniques*, IX (1954), 26–36.

3. *Georg Büchner: Die dramatische Ausdruckswelt*, p. 117.

4. "Some Letters," trans. Maurer, p. 50.

5. *Georg Büchners "Leonce und Lena": Ein Lustspiel der Langeweile* (Heidelberg, 1961), pp. 14–27 and *passim.*

4—*Lenz: Internal Drama and the Form of Fiction*

1. For an easily accessible copy of the diary see Herbert Thiele, "Georg Büchners 'Lenz' als sprachliches Kunstwerk," *Deutschunterricht*, VIII (1956), 63–70.

2. *Zwischen Klassik und Moderne* (Stuttgart, 1958), pp. 131–32, 423–24.

3. *A Portrait of the Artist as a Young Man* (New York, 1956), p. 215.

4. *Das Bild in der Dichtung* (Marburg, 1939), II, 255.

5. "William Faulkner: 1897–1962," *Sewanee Review*, LXXI (1963), 162.

6. Although Büchner may have planned to continue the story past this point, it seems likely that he intended these words as a conclusion, especially since his source does not continue Lenz' story any further. There is, however, an obvious break in Büchner's narrative just before Lenz is about to be taken to Strasbourg; Oberlin's diary, at any rate, includes several pages of events at this point which Büchner made no use of. If the story is to be taken as a fragment, the unfinished portion would seem to be this break and not, I think, an addition to the final words in the manuscript. It is even possible that Büchner had no intention of filling in this break—the story seems a unified whole as it stands—but never got around to making a transition from Lenz' fall from the window to his departure for Strasbourg.

7. *Das Bild in der Dichtung*, II, 259–60.

8. Bergemann, p. 405.

5—*Woyzeck: Towards Drama as Poetic Image*

1. "Wortgewebe, Sinngefüge und 'Idee' in Büchners 'Woyzeck,'" pp. 521–57.

2. "Volkslied und Verseinlage in den Dramen Büchners," *Deutsche Vierteljahrsschrift*, XXXV (1961), 569.

3. *Ibid.*, pp. 581–89.

4. *Wheel of Fire* (London, 1930), pp. 3–6.

5. "Zum Menschenbild Georg Büchners," pp. 16–17.

6. For reprints of the relevant portions of Clarus' report, see Walther Kupsch, *Wozzeck: Ein Beitrag zum Schaffen Georg Büchners* (Berlin, 1920), pp. 17–28, and Hans Winkler, *Georg Büchners "Woyzeck"* (Greifswald, 1925), pp. 95–111. Winkler also mentions several other cases from which Büchner may well have drawn some details (pp. 111–17).

7. Kupsch, pp. 27–28.

8. For an elaborate and conclusive demonstration that Büchner did not intend to have Woyzeck brought to trial or executed, see Wolfgang Martens, "Der Barbier in Büchners 'Woyzeck,'" *Zeitschrift für deutsche Philologie*, LXXIX (1960), 361–83. Carl Richard Mueller's recent translation of Büchner (*Complete Plays and Prose*—New York, 1963), which did not reach me until this manuscript was complete, unfortunately fails to take cognizance of Martens' work; as

a result, his version of *Woyzeck* not only culminates in Woyzeck's arrest, but it also puts into Woyzeck's mouth a group of speeches (pp. 129–30) from an early draft which Büchner in all likelihood did not intend for his title character. For a discussion of the misunderstanding which underlies Mueller's inclusion of these speeches, see pp. 366–71 of Martens' essay.

9. For various recent discussions of Büchner's probable intentions for a conclusion, see Martens' article cited in the preceding note, pp. 381–82; Krapp, *Der Dialog bei Georg Büchner*, pp. 91–93; and H. van Dam, "Zu Georg Büchners 'Woyzeck,'" *Akzente*, I (1954), 82–99. Martens and Van Dam argue for the drowning scene; Krapp believes that the nature of Büchner's dramaturgy renders any such speculations useless.

10. For an analysis of Büchner's use of dialect, see Winkler, pp. 219–23.

11. *Das Groteske* (Oldenburg, 1957), p. 99.

12. In Winkler, pp. 118–21.

13. Bergemann, p. 572.

14. "Zur Karikatur in der Dichtung Büchners (Woyzecks Hauptmann)," *Germanisch-Romanische Monatsschrift*, VIII (1958), 67–68.

15. *Dantons Tod and Woyzeck*, ed. Jacobs (Manchester, 1954), pp. 142–43.

16. Kupsch, p. 21.

17. Bergemann, p. 396.

18. In *Das deutsche Drama*, ed. Benno von Wiese, II, 91.

6—Forebears, Descendants, and Contemporary Kin: Büchner and Literary Tradition

1. "Über das Poetische und Artistische," *Stücke* (Frankfort, 1959), XI, 216.

2. Walter Höllerer's analysis of *The Soldiers* (in Von Wiese's *Das deutsche Drama*, I, 127–46) includes some penetrating remarks on those aspects of Lenz' work which anticipate Büchner's.

3. Bergemann, pp. 553, 400.

4. *Ibid.*, p. 523.

5. Quoted in Ernst Johann, *Georg Büchner in Selbstzeugnissen und Bilddokumenten* (Hamburg, 1958), p. 166.

6. Wolfgang Kayser defines several parallels between Büchner and Wedekind in their use of the grotesque in *Das Groteske*, pp. 141–43.

7. Adapted from Willi Reich's analysis of the opera, "A Guide to *Wozzeck*," *Musical Quarterly*, XXXVIII (1952), 1–20. For a very different critical approach to the opera, see the chapter on *Wozzeck* and *The Rake's Progress* in Joseph Kerman's *Opera as Drama* (New York, 1959), pp. 219–49.

8. See Berg's note on the opera reprinted with Reich's analysis, pp. 20–21.

9. " 'Ulysses,' Order, and Myth," in *Criticism: The Foundations of Modern Literary Judgment*, ed. Mark Schorer, Josephine Miles, and Gordon McKenzie (New York, 1948), p. 270.

10. Translated by Eric Bentley and Desmond Vesey, *The Modern Theatre* (New York, 1955), I, 168.

11. "Discovering the Theatre," trans. Leonard C. Pronko, *Tulane Drama Review*, IV (1959), 6.

12. Martin Esslin, in his study of the contemporary "absurd" drama, cites especially *Leonce and Lena* as an ancestor of this movement (*The Theatre of the Absurd*—New York, 1961—pp. 238–39).

13. *Waiting for Godot* (New York, 1954), p. 52.

14. "Georg Büchner's *Danton's Death*," p. 148.

15. "Some Letters," trans. Maurer, p. 54.

16. Bergemann, p. 390.

17. *Ibid.*, p. 556.

18. See, for instance, the echoes and parallels cited by Heinrich Vogeley, *Georg Büchner und Shakespeare* (Marburg, 1934), pp. 30–51; Rudolf Majut, "Some Literary Affiliations of Georg Büchner with England," *Modern Language Review*, L (1955), 30–32; and Bergemann, p. 672. There is no evidence that Büchner read Shakespeare in English. His echoes are based on the standard German translation by Ludwig Tieck and August Wilhelm Schlegel.

19. *Letters*, ed. H. E. Rollins (Cambridge, Mass., 1958), I, 387.

20. See, for example, Knight's study of the imagery of *Lear*, "The Lear Universe," in *Wheel of Fire*, pp. 194–226, or Empson's study of the functions of a single word in the play, "Fool in *Lear*," in *The Structure of Complex Words* (London, 1951), pp. 125–57.

21. Bergemann, p. 408.

22. *Ibid.*

23. Walter Höllerer, in *Zwischen Klassik und Moderne,* has made the best attempt thus far to define a common ground between Büchner and his contemporary writers in German, above all, Grabbe, Heine, Raimund, Nestroy, and Büchner's fellow Hessian writer, Ernst Elias Niebergall. (See the chapter on Büchner, pp. 100–42, and also pp. 36, 37, 63, 65, 67, 68, 80, 85, 151, 168, 169, 176, 178–79, 184, 189, 198–99.) Among the features which Höllerer distinguishes as common to most of these figures are a persistent skepticism, a fusion of wit and pathos, and the development of peculiarly terse ways of expression. Höllerer's fine argument does not deny the fact that Büchner has spoken to our age with a greater degree of contemporaneity than any of these other writers.

24. Despite his antipathies to German Romanticism, in a few respects his work represents a continuation of the aims and methods of this movement. *Leonce and Lena,* in its wordplay, its concern with boredom, and its attempt to re-evoke the world of Shakespearean comedy, has something in common with Clemens Brentano's charming but impossibly diffuse comedy *Ponce de Leon* (1803), which, exactly thirty-five years before, had been submitted to the same competition for which Büchner prepared his play. Gutzkow, in fact, pointed out the parallel between the two plays in his memorial tribute to Büchner (in Bergemann, p. 595). Büchner's attempts, in *Danton's Death* and *Woyzeck,* to fuse comic and tragic elements and to break down the conventions of German Classical drama were among the central aims of the German Romantic school, which, however, was unable to produce a dramatist who could realize these aims. The apocalyptic grandeur with which the prisoners voice their despair in *Danton's Death* has something in common with the tone of *Night Watches* (1804) by Bonaventura (*pseud.*), one of a number of German Romantic works which anticipate the nihilistic attitudes of Büchner's characters. The grotesqueness of figures such as the captain and doctor in *Woyzeck* perhaps owes something to the grotesque characterizations of E. T. A. Hoffmann, with whose poetic world Büchner momentarily identified himself in one of his letters to his fiancée (in Bergemann, pp. 379–80). The sense of fullness with which Büchner characterizes the landscape in

parts of *Lenz* ("he stretched himself out and lay on the earth, dug his way into the All") is perhaps the only aspect of his story which would keep it from being mistaken for a work of our own century. For studies of the relationship of *Leonce and Lena* with German Romanticism, see Armin Renker, *Georg Büchner und das Lustspiel der Romantik* (Berlin, 1924) and Gustav Beckers' *Georg Büchners "Leonce und Lena,"* pp. 73–102.

BIBLIOGRAPHY

[This list includes only those books and essays on Büchner which seem to me particularly informative and/or stimulating. Titles of exceptional interest are marked with an asterisk.]

*Baumann, Gerhart. *Georg Büchner: Die dramatische Ausdruckswelt*. Göttingen, 1961

Baxandall, Lee. "Georg Büchner's *Danton's Death*," *Tulane Drama Review*, VI (1962), 136–49.

Beckers, Gustav. *Georg Büchners "Leonce und Lena": Ein Lustspiel der Langeweile*. Heidelberg, 1961.

Bergemann, Fritz. "Georg Büchner-Schrifttum seit 1937," *Deutsche Vierteljahrsschrift*, XXV (1951), 112–21.

*———. Documents, afterword, and index to his edition of Büchner's *Werke und Briefe*. Wiesbaden, 1958.

Dam, Hermann van. "Zu Georg Büchners 'Woyzeck,'" *Akzente*, I (1954), 82–99.

Duvignaud, Jean. *Georg Büchner: Dramaturge*. Paris, 1954.

*Fink, G.-L. "Volkslied und Verseinlage in den Dramen Büchners," *Deutsche Vierteljahrsschrift*, XXXV (1961), 558–93.

Frisch, Max. "Emigranten: Rede zur Verleihung des Georg Büchner-Preises, 1958," *Moderna Språk*, LIII (1959), 243–54.

Furness, N. A. "Georg Büchner's Translations of Victor Hugo," *Modern Language Review*, LI (1956), 49–54.

Gravier, Maurice. "Georg Büchner et Alfred de Musset," *Orbus Litterarum*, IX (1954), 29–44.

Gundolf, Friedrich. "Georg Büchner," in *Romantiker*. Berlin, 1930, pp. 375–95.

Guthke, Karl S. In *Geschichte und Poetik der deutschen Tragikomödie*. Göttingen, 1961, pp. 179–97.

Gutzkow, Karl. "Georg Büchner" (1837), reprinted in Bergemann's edition, pp. 589–95.

Hamburger, Michael. "Georg Büchner," in *Reason and Energy*. London, 1957, pp. 179–208.

Hauch, Edward Franklin. "The Reviviscence of Georg Büchner," *PMLA*, LIV (1929), 892–900.

*Höllerer, Walter. "*Dantons Tod*," in *Das deutsche Drama vom Barock bis zur Gegenwart*, ed. Benno von Wiese. Düsseldorf, 1962, II, 65–88.

*———. "Georg Büchner," in *Zwischen Klassik und Moderne: Lachen und Weinen in der Dichtung einer Übergangszeit*. Stuttgart, 1958, pp. 100–142.

Jacobs, Margaret. Introduction and notes to her edition of Büchner's *Dantons Tod and Woyzeck*. Manchester, 1954.

Johann, Ernst. *Georg Büchner in Selbstzeugnissen und Bilddokumenten*. Hamburg, 1958.

Kayser, Wolfgang. In *Das Groteske*. Oldenburg, 1957, pp. 95–102.

Knight, A. H. J. *Georg Büchner*. Oxford, 1951.

Krapp, Helmut. *Der Dialog bei Georg Büchner*. Darmstadt, 1958.

Lukács, Georg. "Der faschistisch verfälschte und der wirkliche Georg Büchner," in *Deutsche Realisten des neunzehnten Jahrhunderts*. Berlin, 1952, pp. 66–88.

Majut, Rudolf. "Georg Büchner and Some English Thinkers," *Modern Language Review*, XLVIII (1953), 310–22.

———. "Some Literary Affiliations of Georg Büchner with England," *Modern Language Review*, L (1955), 29–43.

———. *Studien um Büchner: Untersuchungen zur Geschichte der problematischen Natur*. Berlin, 1932.

*Martens, Wolfgang. "Der Barbier in Büchners 'Woyzeck' (Zugleich ein Beitrag zur Motivgeschichte der Barbiersfigur)," *Zeitschrift für deutsche Philologie*, LXXIX (1960), 361–83.

*———. "Ideologie und Verzweiflung: Religiöse Motive in Büchners Revolutionsdrama," *Euphorion*, LIV (1960), 83–108.

*———. "Zum Menschenbild Georg Büchners: 'Woyzeck' und die Marionszene in 'Dantons Tod,'" *Wirkendes Wort*, VIII (1957), 13–20.

*———. "Zur Karikatur in der Dichtung Büchners (Woyzecks Hauptmann)," *Germanisch-Romanische Monatsschrift*, XXXIX, n. f. VIII (1958), 64–71.

*Mautner, Franz H. "Wortgewebe, Sinngefüge und 'Idee' in Büchners 'Woyzeck,'" *Deutsche Vierteljahrsschrift*, XXXV (1961), 521–57.

May, Kurt. "*Woyzeck*," in *Das deutsche Drama vom Barock bis zur Gegenwart*. Düsseldorf, 1962, II, 89–100.

Mayer, Hans. *Georg Büchner und seine Zeit*. Berlin, 1960.

Oppel, Horst. "Stand und Aufgaben der Büchner-Forschung," *Euphorion*, XLIX (1955), 91–109.

*———. *Die tragische Dichtung Georg Büchners*. Stuttgart, 1951.

Peacock, Ronald. "A Note on Georg Büchner's Plays," *German Life and Letters*, n. s. X (1957), 189–97.

Plard, Henri. "A propos de *Leonce und Lena:* Musset et Büchner," *Etudes germaniques*, IX (1954), 26–36.

Pongs, Hermann. "Büchners 'Lenz,'" in *Das Bild in der Dichtung*. Marburg, 1939, II, 254–65.

Renker, Armin. *Georg Büchner und das Lustspiel der Romantik: Eine Studie über "Leonce und Lena."* Berlin, 1924.

Rosenberg, Ralph P. "Georg Büchner's Early Reception in America," *Journal of English and Germanic Philology*, XLIV (1945), 270–73.

Schonauer, Franz. "Das Drama und die Geschichte: Versuch über Georg Büchner," *Deutsche Rundschau*, LXXXVII (1960), 533–50.

Schwarz, Egon. "Tod und Witz im Werke Georg Büchners," *Monatshefte für den deutschen Unterricht*, XLVI (1954), 123–36.

Sengle, Friedrich. "Grabbe und Büchner," in *Das deutsche Geschichtsdrama*. Stuttgart, 1952.

Strohl, Jean. *Lorenz Oken und Georg Büchner: Zwei Gestalten aus der Übergangszeit von Naturphilosophie zu Naturwissenschaft*. Zurich, 1936.

Strudthoff, Ingeborg. *Die Rezeption Georg Büchners durch das deutsche Theater*. Berlin, 1957.

Thieberger, Richard. Critical apparatus to his edition of Büchner's *La Mort de Danton*. Paris, 1953.

Viëtor, Karl. *Georg Büchner als Politiker*. Berne, 1939.

*———. *Georg Büchner: Politik, Dichtung, Wissenschaft*. Berne, 1949.

Vogeley, Heinrich. *Georg Büchner und Shakespeare*. Marburg, 1934.

Wiese, Benno von. "Georg Büchner: Die Tragödie des Nihilismus," in *Die deutsche Tragödie von Lessing bis Hebbel.* Hamburg, 1948, II, 309–33.

———. "Die Religion Büchners und Hebbels," in *Hebbel-Jahrbuch.* Heide-in-Holstein, 1959.

Winkler, Hans. *Georg Büchners "Woyzeck."* Greifswald, 1925.

INDEX

helpless stagnancy